Divine

BEINGS

Divine Beings:

The Spiritual Lives and Lessons of Animals

Cara Gubbins, PhD

www.CaraGubbins.com

This book is dedicated to all the animals in the world

– thank you for being you.

Table of Contents

Introduction

Do you ever wonder what your pets are trying to say to you? Do you wish you knew what happened to your pet after s/he died? Do you find yourself wondering what animals at the zoo are thinking or what it's like to be a wild animal?

Many of us, especially pet owners, instinctively feel that animals' lives are deeper and more meaningful than what conventional science and religion tell us. Different animals, even brothers and sisters in the same family, behave differently and seem to have different personalities. Our animals give us significant looks and react to words we say to them. They know when we're coming home or when we're sick or sad. They respond to us and we respond to them. Something seems to be going on inside their cute little heads!

As a wildlife biologist, I have spent over twenty years studying the behavior of a variety of animals from lizards to penguins to dolphins. Through it all, I wondered, "What goes on in their minds?" Now as a spiritual Animal Intuitive, I am able to communicate directly with animals and get insight into my long-standing question.

As a dog owner, I've lived with my own pets and been deeply touched by their friendships. My first dog gave me deep comfort and companionship after my parents divorced. My current dog is my constant companion and has been since my graduate student days writing my PhD dissertation. By piecing together animals' answers to their peoples' questions during intuitive readings, I've come to understand that animals and humans choose to be together in this life and both parties have something to learn from the other. The lessons taught and learned seem to be similar within species and different between species. For instance, dogs are all about giving and receiving love. Cats are more about balancing affection and independence. Our connections with our pets can be strong, transcending this life and our physical existence.

As a spiritual biologist, I've approached animals over the past year with both love and curiosity. Each time I connect intuitively with an animal I sense not just the animal's message, but I also get to feel a bit of its soul. It is a sacred honor to have that level of trust and intimacy with another creature. I've put my enduring general question "What goes on in their minds?" into three specific questions that I've asked dogs, cats, dolphins, whales, lions, owls, bats and more. Through this process, I've learned that animals really are here to learn their own spiritual lessons alongside humans. By understanding their reality and their point of view, we can better understand our own lives and make better decisions for ourselves, our families, our animals, and our planet.

The writing of this book was the culmination of a lifetime journey for me to uncover and live my spiritual truth. I want to take you along on my journey, so you can make your own journey, too.

Part One is my story in three chapters. The first chapter details my discovery of my psychic skills as a child, my rejection of that ability as a slightly older child, and the way I am (finally!) celebrating this gift as an adult. The second chapter recounts my journey from spiritually precocious child to atheist teenager to spiritually integrated adult. The third chapter details the marriage I made inside myself between my spiritual and scientific aspects and how those play out together in the spiritual biology process I created during my journey this year and in this book. This section gives great background for the animal chapters in the following section. It will help you understand why I chose this project, why I chose my questions, and why I chose to scientifically test my spiritual beliefs.

Part Two includes ten chapters with the messages from the many animals I encountered over the past year. Each chapter focuses on one species and includes the symbolism of the animals in mythology and worldwide spiritual traditions, their natural history, and their responses to my three questions (What is your spiritual lesson? What is your spiritual gift? What message do you have for humans?). Each chapter also includes my subjective intuitive experience of bringing my energetic awareness into the form of each animal species so that you can vicariously experience what it's like to be in their skin, to feel what they feel, see what they see, and know what they know.

Part Three is about the effects of connecting deeply with such a wide variety of animals. What do I do differently now? What has this journey meant to me? How have I changed as a result of my soul encounters with these animals? This chapter recounts the lessons I learned personally from each animal I met along my journey. This chapter examines the implications of a new spiritual paradigm that every being is a divine being. This chapter is a call to action to the reader, an invitation to each of us to live our truth, to allow our actions and words to be guided by our spiritual truths.

Part One: My Story

Dreams Come True

As far back as I can remember, I've always loved animals. In fact, when I was three years old and living in a Chicago suburb, my nickname was "Seal Baby," because I spent so much time swimming underwater pretending to be a seal or a dolphin or a whale whenever my family went to the pool or beach. I loved the pressure of the water on my skin and the buoyancy lifting me and how quiet it would get when my ears were submerged. I also loved the graceful, sinuous way I moved through the water as I swam, my long hair trailing behind me like a mermaid, and the way I could see myself in the undulating silvery mirror of the underside of the water's surface.

When I was six, back before cable TV, Animal Planet, and 5,000 on-demand television channels, Sunday night was our family's television night because that's when the nature programs were on. We started with Wild Kingdom. The host, Marlin Perkins, would narrate as his sidekick, Jim, wrestled an anaconda or an alligator or a water buffalo. Before Jim's heroics, we got up-close views of wild animals in their natural habitats all over the world. I was in heaven. But the highlight of the night for me was the next show, "The Undersea World of Jacques Cousteau." The swamps and savannahs of Wild Kingdom were great, but for a "Seal Baby" like me, seeing the underwater animals was like being transported to nirvana. This is when I decided that I wanted to be a marine biologist when I grew up.

My dream stayed with me through elementary school and middle school and even into high school. One evening when I was a sophomore in high school, my mom took me to see a movie in San Francisco. It was an independent film made by a local filmmaker and his wife who was a biologist. The film was about their research project studying communication between people and wild Atlantic spotted dolphins in the Bahamas. And they were looking for volunteers. I saved up the money from my job at a coffee house and paid half my way to volunteer on their boat for a week that summer. My mom donated the other half to my cause. I was going to be a marine biologist!

I flew from San Francisco to Miami and took a cab to a little marina in Miami Beach. The research boat was a modified PT boat used for private tours and excursions. A group of scientists had rented it for the summer, sailing back and forth to the Bahamas each week with a new group of volunteers. In the Bahamas, we anchored at a place called the Little Sand Banks, which is miles from any piece of land. When you get out there, all you can see in any direction is blue ocean and blue sky. The sandy bottom is perfectly white and the water is perfectly clear and only about twenty to thirty feet deep, depending on the tides.

Every day, we'd sit on the decks scanning the horizon and waiting for dolphins to swim by. When they did, the scientists quickly donned their snorkeling gear, jumped in the water and did their research. Right behind them, the volunteers suited up and jumped in the water, too. Our job was to identify individuals by their spotting patterns and nicks and scars on their bodies, drawing the patterns on a plastic slate with a pencil tethered to it with surgical tubing that we carried with us.

On the day before we were to sail home, a huge group of at least 30 dolphins surrounded the boat. Everyone raced into the water. Three dolphins singled me out and stayed with me the entire time. One swam on my left, one on my right and the third was underneath me. We swam as a unit, up to the surface to breathe, down to the sandy bottom, circling in and around each other.

As I swam shoulder to shoulder with the dolphins, I turned my head to the right and caught the eye of that dolphin. She looked directly back at me and our eyes locked. There was such depth in that deep, brown eye that I knew that she could see through me, see into me, see into the depths of my being. I felt like she was looking into my soul. Gazing into her eye, I got lost in her. I felt like I, too, could see deep into the depths of her soul. In a flash, I knew there was much more to her than I had ever imagined. This dolphin was more than flesh and blood swimmingly unconsciously through the ocean. She had a soul. I looked in her eye and saw myself there. There was no difference between us. We just came in different forms. Long seconds passed and I began to run out of breath, but I fought it. My stomach tightened and I clamped down on my snorkel, willing my cells to suck just a little more oxygen from my red blood cells or to just live without oxygen for a while. I didn't want this moment to end. Somehow she knew I needed air and she rose to the surface. I followed. We took a quick breath and the spell was broken; the moment was over. The other two dolphins zoomed in front of us, inviting us to chase them as they spiraled down toward the white sandy bottom.

One dolphin picked up a piece of seaweed in her mouth and trailed it behind her, dropping it in front of the second dolphin, who dragged it on his pectoral fin. I followed along like someone's slower kid sister trying to get into the big kids' game. Then the seaweed was boring and one of the dolphins used his echolocation to buzz a fish buried under the surface of the sand. We surfaced to breathe and dove again.

I have no idea how long I swam like that with them. Time stood still and nothing else existed. Finally, I noticed that I didn't see any other people or dolphins in the water around us. I surfaced and looked for the boat, which was a couple hundred yards away. I could see that everyone else was out of the water and the big group of dolphins was heading away from the boat and away from me and my three dolphins. Under the water, the three dolphins were frozen, waiting for me. I sank back underwater and re-joined them. We swam together, but now they were trying to catch up to their group and I lagged behind. They stopped and looked back at me, waiting. I caught up to them and they started quickly toward their group.

I fell behind again, watching them swim into the distance. They stopped and looked back at me one last time, waiting for me to catch up. Every cell in my body wanted to follow them. But I knew that I had to return to the boat. Reluctantly, I started swimming my retreat. Halfway to the boat, I glimpsed back over my shoulder just as the trio disappeared into the dark blue ocean.

Back on the boat, I knew that I had found my calling. I loved all animals, but dolphins were in my soul now. I wanted to learn everything there was to know about them. My mind was made up: I would go home, finish high school, go to college, and get a Ph.D.

And that's exactly what I did. I graduated from high school two years later, in 1982. In 1987, I received my bachelor's degree in General Biology from the University of California San Diego. In 1993, after studying the development of the social behavior of captive bottlenose dolphins calves for my thesis, I received my master's degree in Animal Behavior and Physiology from San Francisco State University. And, I graduated from the University of Nevada Reno with a PhD in Ecology, Evolution and Conservation Biology in May 2000, almost exactly twenty years after my swim with the three dolphins in the Bahamas. For my dissertation I studied the behavior and social structure of wild bottlenose dolphins in the saltwater creeks and sounds of coastal South Carolina. During the course of my six years of study, I had lived in Reno for two years, South Carolina for two years and, when my boyfriend got a job in Tampa, I had spent the last two years of my degree in Florida, analyzing my data and writing my dissertation on the opposite side of the country from my school and my advisor.

Back home in Florida after graduation, I thought to myself, "Now what?" My fellow graduates were sending resumes to dozens of universities, applying for research and teaching jobs. I had a single job offer: to study the behavior and social structure of wild bottlenose dolphins in Tampa Bay as a postdoctoral research scientist. I turned it down. I had achieved my goal, I was a marine biologist, but it felt empty. I just couldn't see myself doing the same thing all over again that I had just done for my PhD. I wanted change. I wanted a new adventure. But I had no idea what it was. Professionally speaking, I was drifting.

At the time, our Australian shepherd puppy, Iko, was a year old and she demanded long walks twice a day. Every evening after dinner, my boyfriend Chris and I would walk her around our neighborhood and talk about whatever was going on in our lives. Quite often the subject was my career. I was trying to figure out what to do next because everything I had done in the last nineteen years was moving me toward being a marine biologist and now that I was one, I wasn't sure anymore that I wanted to be one.

One humid fall evening as we were nearing our home on our nightly walk, Chris said to me, with more than a hint of frustration in his voice, "Well, what do you *want* to do?" Something in his tone jarred me and I answered before I was aware of what I was saying, the words "I want to be a psychic" popping right out of my mouth. "Oh. Then do that," was his nonchalant response. My forehead furrowed, my eyebrows raised, my head even comically tilted to the side. "How the hell would I do that?!" I thought to myself. Psychics are born not made. How do you just go out and become a psychic? Plus, I just spent the last nineteen years training to be a scientist. More than half my life had been spent learning how to do science! I had a PhD! This was just crazy talk! Where had those words even come from?

But those words haunted me. They had felt so true, so right. That really was what I wanted to do, but how to do it? I had no clue. At Christmastime, we visited our families out West and one afternoon I found myself driving alone through the rolling hills of coastal northern California. To my right, the grassy hills rose gently like undulating green waves bravely offering themselves up to be consumed by the darker green trees in the distance. To my left, the valley lay flat and open for a few hundred yards before being swallowed by another towering forest. A red, wooden fence ran along the road, defining the pastures for different species of livestock.

As I drove past the second pasture, my eye was drawn to three horses spread out in the field, casually eating grass. My chest tightened; my throat constricted. Tears streamed down my face. Deep inside me was an ache I had never felt before. I wanted to talk to those horses. It felt like my soul needed to talk to them. Longing was pouring out of me. What could we say to each other? What could they tell me about their lives, their views of reality? I didn't know but I wanted, no I needed, to find out.

Now, I'm not a horse person. I'm a marine biologist and, if I'm any kind of domesticated animal person, I'm a dog person. I'm not a horse person. I did not play with horses as a little girl and I had ridden a horse once in my life – and I had gotten hives all over my legs because I was allergic. I would have to say that I have no special connection to horses and, ever since the hives incident, I had given horses a lot of space. So this spontaneous reaction was mystifying to me. I could understand wanting to talk to dolphins or whales, but horses?! Come on!

Then, a little light bulb went off inside my head. I was going to talk to whales. I was going to figure out what they were saying in their songs. I remembered. When I was six that was the reason I had wanted to become a marine biologist. That was my dream. Or was it? Now that the cosmic gates into my childhood dreams and desires had opened, the memories flooded back and I realized that that was only part of it. Before Jacques Cousteau, there had been another figure I had wanted to emulate: Dr. Doolittle. I wanted to walk with the animals, talk with the animals, just like he did. Those three horses were small dots in my rearview mirror as I uncovered the real dream of my life: to talk to animals. All animals. And I wanted to do it like he did – causally, like it was a totally normal, natural thing to do. And I would help the animals, like Dr. Doolittle did. Not medically, but I would be their messenger, their interpreter. I would be able to tell other people what the animals were trying to say to them. I would be Dr. Doolittle. This was my dream as a five year old. The whole thing came flooding back to me, the dream, the ideas, the feelings, the excitement, the fun of it. This was my first dream, even before I had dreamed of being a marine biologist.

I had found my dream, but I had to live with it unfulfilled for ten years. I had this yearning inside of me and I didn't know what to do with it. I knew this was what I wanted, but I had no idea of how to pursue it. If there had been a graduate course in psychic communication with animals, I would have aced it. I would have applied to the program, taken the classes, done all the work – just as I had done for my bachelor's degree and my master's degree and my doctoral degree on the way to becoming a scientist. But this, this was foreign to me. This was airy-fairy and mystical and touchy-feely and all those things that you just can't get a grip on. There was no school, no teacher, no expert to tell me what to do. I was lost.

But I was not idle. Chris and I got married and I got to work writing a book incorporating everything I had ever learned about dolphins. *The Dolphins of Hilton Head* was published two years later, in 2002. This would have been the biggest, proudest event of my life so far except that my daughter was born a few months earlier and that eclipsed the excitement in any other area of my life. And, as it tends to do, life went on. When Lexi was two, we moved back to California, settling in a small college town in the north part of the state. I began teaching biology at the local community college and life was very full. Zane was born the following summer (in 2005) and the demands of motherhood and teaching consumed most of my energy for the next five years.

We still took Iko for a walk most nights after dinner, and if we were outside when the stars began to appear, I always wished on the first star. My wish always went like this "Star light, star bright, first star I see tonight. I wish I may, I wish I might, get this wish I wish tonight: I wish I could talk to animals." Nearly ten years after my epiphany driving through northern California, my dream was still bubbling around inside of me and I still had no idea what to do about it, or how to make it come true. I felt kind of like a dope.

Here I was an intelligent, successful woman, a published author and a college professor and the mother of two beautiful kids, reduced to secretly wishing on a star to make her crazy childhood dream come true. That stuff doesn't really work . . . does it? Well, it was about the only hope I had for years. And then I learned about USM.

The University of Santa Monica offers graduate degrees in Spiritual Psychology. Their program teaches well-known psychological theories and tools in a new context to help students evolve spiritually. As part of the curriculum, students create a second year project of their choice. This project is a chance for students to "make their dreams come true," as it states on the school's website. A flame was ignited in me when I read those words. Because I still had my dream. It seemed a silly, impossible dream to me. But I was 45 years old. I didn't want to die with my dream unrealized inside of me. If there was any way to make it happen, I wanted to try it. I wanted with all my heart to become Dr. Doolittle. This was my chance. It felt like my last chance. I grasped desperately at this lifeline and enrolled in the program.

A week after I got accepted, I was window shopping in town when I saw a sign for a year-long class designed to open up people's natural intuitive or psychic abilities. It started in a month and I signed up on the spot. This was the key to unlocking my ability to talk to animals. This was the key to unlocking my dream. I could feel it. I completed the psychic training class in June 2010. The psychic program even had a class devoted to communicating intuitively with animals. Towards the end of the program, three dogs came to class and my classmates and I asked them questions and compared notes. I wasn't very good at it. Although I had gotten a few answers that were verified by the owner as being correct, my classmates seemed to get more information than I did. My teacher told us that most people are happy if they learn one or even two things about their animal from a reading. If you could do that, you were doing a good job. But I wanted more than that. I wanted to be Dr. Doolittle. Undeterred by my poor results in class, I decided to embark on my own course of study in intuitive animal communication. I decided to become an expert. I checked books out of the library; I bought books at the bookstore. I read them all. I did the exercises the authors suggested. All to no avail. I was still hit or miss with my attempts to talk to animals and on top of that, I was afraid to tell people what I was doing in order to ask to practice with their pets.

All that changed in September 2010. One night after the kids went to bed, I was having an argument with my husband. I felt like he was acting like he didn't believe me about something and he said he was just being complete, offering a different point of view, playing the devil's advocate. "I'm so mad at you!" I said - and suddenly I realized that I wasn't mad at him at all, I was actually mad at my dad. Our argument had triggered a buried anger inside of me that was coming to the surface. As a child I had been mad at my dad for not believing something I had said but I had had no way to articulate it at the time.

As I learned at USM, this is called an incomplete Gestalt. According to this theory, I had had an emotion that I had suppressed at a young age, and every time a similar interaction occurred, this emotion was triggered in order to complete the incomplete interaction. But it takes a very aware person to recognize this phenomenon. Luckily, we had been learning about and practicing the skills to recognize and complete incomplete Gestalts at school. My anger at my dad was coming to the surface now to be released and healed. I apologized to my husband for yelling at him, "I'm sorry, I'm actually mad at my dad," I said in a bit of a daze. "I felt like he didn't believe me and he asked who could verify what I was telling him."

Then, in another flash of insight, I realized that I was mad not at my dad but at myself. Through that childhood interaction with my dad, I had created an unconscious belief that no one believes me. "Oh, wait," I told my husband, "I'm actually mad at myself." I'm sure he was getting very confused very quickly! I was mad at myself for thinking that no one believes me. It was a stunning series of revelations to make in a matter of a few minutes and it took all the fight out of our argument.

My husband and I resolved our differences and made up. I forgave myself for creating that belief and buying into the misconception that I wasn't worthy of being believed by myself or other people. I realized that I was trustworthy. I was honest. I was believable. My unconscious belief was brought to the surface and it had melted under my scrutiny, to be replaced with the truth that I am believable and trustworthy. A feeling of peace and exhilaration flooded me.

The next day, I was visiting my friend Ellery. I hadn't seen her in several months and we were planning to have tea and catch up with each other. Ellery is a former nurse now on disability due to a debilitating on-the-job accident at the hospital where she used to work. She has sandy brown hair and soft, brown eyes and the sweetest, most patient disposition of anyone I know. She also happens to be a psychic that is able to talk to animals. I told her about my dream to be Dr. Doolittle and how hard I was working on it and how I wasn't very good, and I didn't think I could really do it, but could she maybe help me out and teach me how to do it? She looked at me with disbelief and said, "Really? I thought you were already doing that? That's who you are." I looked at her blankly. She thought I could do this? She thought I was already doing this? She thought this was just part of who I am? Huh, that's weird, I thought to myself.

Before I could even respond, she matter-of-factly said, "Ask Bear why she's mad at my husband Cale." So I did. I cleared my mind, looked at her cute, little Chihuahua with her tan body, big eyes, and white shield on her chest, and sent the thought to her, "Why are you mad at Cale?" Immediately I saw a picture in my mind of Bear standing on a pillow on Ellery and Kale's bed, barking and barking and barking at something on the other side of the room. "What are you barking at?" I asked her. I saw a picture of a shadowy figure emerging from the master bathroom. It was big and dark and scary. It was Cale coming to bed after turning out the bathroom light. I described what I saw to Ellery and she said, "That's exactly right. Bear has been mad at him for 3 days for turning off the light before he came to bed. What can Cale do to make it up to her?" I sent this question to Bear in my mind and immediately saw a picture of Cale at the kitchen table lowering a bowl of milk to the floor in front of Bear. I relayed my vision to Ellery and she said, "Yeah, Bear loves to drink Cale's cereal milk after he's done eating the cereal. Thanks, I'll tell Cale what he needs to do."

Holy crap! I was really doing this! And it wasn't just brief impressions; it was accurate information that was verifiable and real. It came to me fully and naturally, as if I'd been doing this my whole life. Whoa! I realized that what had been holding me back from tapping into my natural ability to do this was my subconscious belief that no one would believe me. Once I cleared that, I was free to do what I wanted to do and actually become Dr. Doolittle. From that day on, I have been able to talk to animals.

Before that day, I had also held the mistaken belief that intuitive (or psychic) information isn't verifiable or objective. I proved this belief false, too. Because we thought it would be fun, Ellery and I decided to have weekly "field trips" to practice talking to different kinds of animals. Together we have talked to dozens of birds, insects, mammals and reptiles. When working together this way, we each work alone, asking our own questions of the animals or focusing in on our own intuitive information and awareness. Then we compare notes after each of us has finished. Over the several months that we did this, we found that we had about 90% overlap in the information that we get from animals. And in that 10% of difference, it was usually only slightly different but completely compatible with what the other person got.

So, for the last six months I have been living my deepest, earliest childhood dream. I am walking with the animals and talking with the animals. It feels normal and natural and very, well, regular to me. I still do all the normal things that I did before I learned that I can talk with animals. I still take my kids to school each morning like all the other parents in my neighborhood. But now when I go to work, instead of teaching biology to college students, I talk to dogs and cats and horses and goats and donkeys and all kinds of animals and pass their messages on to their people. All those things that I remembered that day driving by the horses in the pasture, everything I wanted to be able to do when I grew up, I am doing. And every day it makes me smile because I realize that dreams really do come true.

Recovering My Spiritual Truth

I was the first of four children born into a Catholic family living the Chicago suburbs. My early childhood was steeped in Catholicism. We went to church each Sunday morning. One of my dad's three brothers is a priest; one of his three sisters is a nun. Three of my great aunts were nuns and one great uncle was a church big wig guy. When I was very young, probably three or four years old, I used to love to try on my aunts' "nun hats" as I called their wimples and look at myself in the mirror. I thought I looked mature and spiritual and beautiful.

I had a natural spiritual knowingness at this time in my life. I felt connected to and loved by God. I could talk to angels. I could talk to God! I think I knew my spiritual truth at this time, even though I didn't have the words to articulate it. If I could have put it to words, I think I would have described it as a feeling of communion, a deep understanding that we are all one and that we are all loved.

Most Sundays while my parents went to mass, I attended Sunday school. I actually liked church and Sunday school when I was little. I loved running my hand along the smooth wooden pews in the church. I loved how the little padded benches folded out from the pew in front of you so you could kneel comfortably when it was time. I loved all the people singing songs together. And in Sunday school, I loved how the teacher said we were God-faring. That made sense to me. I felt like a sailor. Like a seafarer who follows the sea, I was a God-farer, following God.

When I was six years old I learned to read. I loved reading practically more than anything else in the world. I read everything: picture books, road signs, instruction manuals, anything that I saw with words on it. I followed along in the book one Sunday as the Sunday school teacher read a story. She got to a part that said "God fearing" in the book, but she pronounced as "God faring." My stomach hurt and my head spun. I had been betrayed. "God faring" meant "God fearing?!" I was outraged. That didn't make sense to me at all! Why would you ever be afraid of God? These people were idiots! I completely rejected religion at that point and refused to go to church or Sunday school again. (I have no idea how I managed this and what my parents did, but I never went again.)

But somehow, in my six year old brain, I tied spirituality and religion up together and because I rejected Catholicism and Catholics, I felt I had to reject all spirituality. At some point down the road, I don't remember it clearly, I became an atheist. By high school however, I identified myself as "spiritual but not religious." I became interested in Zen Buddhism and eastern philosophies – spiritual traditions that didn't rely on an all-powerful male God that should be feared as their central tenet. Slowly, without any conscious effort, I began working my way back to my natural spiritual truth, that feeling of communion I had when I was a kid – that knowingness before words, that deep understanding that we are all one. My biggest step in that process wouldn't come until years later, when I was thirty years old and I had already completed college and had begun my doctoral studies. And I had to lose the person I loved most in the world to learn the lesson.

****

My mom died on a Tuesday.

She knew she was going to die. First thing that morning she told the four of us kids to stay around her house that day and not go anywhere. She also asked us to contact three of her closest friends and ask them to come over so she could say goodbye to them.

My mom was dying of cancer. I didn't know that when I began my first summer of field work for my PhD dissertation in early June. Two weeks into the season, my youngest brother, called me to say that Mom had lost motor function in her legs the day before and when he had taken her to the hospital they found her Stage IV breast cancer had spread to her brain and several of her bones. He thought the end was near. I dropped my research like a hot potato and flew home immediately to help take care of my mom. She began doing radiation treatments weekly but after a month it was clear that they weren't working and she was getting weaker. Her last chance was an alternative hospital in Mexico with great success healing cancer patients using nutritional therapy. I accompanied her to Tijuana and we stayed for a week before the doctors there sent her home, saying there was nothing more they could do for her. She had been lying in her bed at home for several days and hospice had made a few visits. Now, it was August, a week after her 55th birthday, and today was the day.

She said her goodbyes to her friends in the morning. After that, she had time alone with each of us. First my youngest brother sat and talked with her. Then my sister had her turn. Then my other brother went in. I was the last of her children to sit with her alone. As the oldest sibling, that felt right to me. It was early afternoon when I slowly walked through her bedroom door and approached her in her bed. Her feet were cold and sore, so I gently massaged them and talked to her softly. We had no unfinished business, nothing that needed saying, so I was able to just be with her. We gradually stopped talking and I think she fell asleep. After a while, I sat on a stool next to her bed and lay my hands on her abdomen, my left hand just below her belly button, and my right hand on her solar plexus just below her ribs. I relaxed into the moment, enjoying the quiet communion between us.

With her peaceful breathing guiding me, I drifted into an even more relaxed state, almost like a trance. Through my hands, I could feel her energy softly pulsing through her body. I gazed at the trees in the backyard, their leaves and branches resembling an impressionist painting dappled with patches of greens and browns. I felt so connected to her, it was like I was part of her. I could stay here forever, I thought to myself.

Suddenly, there was a pounding on the soles of my feet. It felt like someone was punching me right in the arches of both feet. Ouch! It hurt! I didn't want to move and I didn't want to take my hands off my mom so I stubbornly remained motionless and brought my attention to my feet. Why was this happening? What should I do? I had no idea, so I just allowed the punching to do what it needed to do and I was simply aware of it. Gradually, the punching stopped and the pain went away. Then it felt like light was streaming up into my feet from somewhere in the middle of the earth. The punching had opened the chakras in the soles of my feet. I didn't know that this was what was happening at the time but this was my first lesson in grounding myself. It was a good thing this happened, because I needed to be grounded for what would happen next. I settled back into the scene, enjoying my last few minutes alone with my mom.

By now I had been with my mom for about an hour and my siblings were getting antsy to see her again. Silently, they filed into the room and took their places standing around my mom. We didn't speak any words; we just looked meaningfully at each other with our eyes. I remained on my stool with my hands on Mom. She was fading. There was silence in the room but there was also a feeling of reverence and grace. I heard birds in the backyard singing. As the four of us watched her over the next 30 minutes or so, my mom's breathing began to slow noticeably. My mind wandered around. I thought about my mom's long battle with cancer and all that we had shared in the last several, scary weeks. I listened to the birds. I watched the trees rustle in a light breeze through the bedroom window. I looked at the sad faces of my brothers and sister as they watched my mom's face. My awareness rested back on my hands and the soft threads of the yellow cotton blanket that was the only barrier between me and my mom's skin.

Then I felt a new sensation. I felt a wave of energy move up through my hands, into my arms and then into my body. It felt like a wave of laughter floating through me. I smiled at the feeling and then it was gone. A moment later another wave of energy followed the same path up my hands and arms and into my body. This wave felt sensual, almost sexy. Then it floated up to the sky and my body just felt like my body again. A third wave of energy moved through me. This one felt strong and powerful, like a strong will or determination. I recognized it as part of my mom's personality. It dawned on me that my mom's spirit was leaving her body, but it wasn't sudden or harsh or painful; it was slow and gentle and gradual and happening in waves. As the waves of my mom continued to pass through me, I felt a great peace settle in my being. The aliveness of her soul was palpable to me. I could feel it moving through me and gathering above us, each wave forming another layer of the whole of her being, never really separated but somehow reunited outside her body.

The waves continued for a few more minutes and I lost myself to them, not even bothering to put words to the sensations but just experiencing them as they were. Then they stopped as mysteriously as they had begun. I looked at my mom's beautiful face with new awe and appreciation. Even in her death she was giving. She had just given me the gift of a lifetime, to share in her essence, to experience the beauty of her transition from form to formlessness. Tears of gratitude and love filled my eyes as I watched her chest move ever so slightly with her next breath. Her soul had left her body. I knew that. The end was very near. We had to wait thirty seconds before hearing the slight rasp of her next inhalation.

Her next breath took even longer and it was shallower when it finally came. From my mom's left side, I looked at my brother standing to the right of her head. We locked eyes and seemed to be asking each other the same question, "Was that the last one?" Our gazes fell to her face and she took one more, slow, shallow breath. That was her last one. The four of us stood silently for a few moments, reeling in the truth of the moment: our mom was gone. We would never see her again. I took a mental photograph of her sweet face lying back on the white pillow. The world stopped spinning in that moment and time stood still for each of us. Tears began to slide down our faces and almost as one, we breathed in deeply the breath of finality that we had been holding back.

There must have been a shift in the energy of the house, because somehow everyone in the house knew that she was gone.

Not a word had been spoken, not a body had moved around my mom's deathbed, but my father and my uncle quietly entered the room. We coalesced into a single form, each of us giving and receiving hugs silently. I walked into the hallway and found Chris and let him hold me for a long time. Then I drifted outside into the front yard. The sun was setting and the warmth of the day radiated from the flowers and trees around me. I felt peaceful and optimistic. There was a lingering tingling in my body from the places my mom's spirit had touched me. Her loving energy still filled me in a way. I couldn't be too sad: she was still alive. Her essence was whole and complete. I hadn't lost *her*; I'd just lost the physical part of her.

I couldn't articulate it at the time, but I had just had my first experience of a human being who was more than a human being. I recognized my mom in the energy that passed through me and that energy was separate from her physical body. She was a spirit that had been inhabiting a body for a while. Okay for 55 years. But she was not her body. She had been a spiritual being having a human experience. By extension, then, I, too, am a spiritual being having a human experience. I am more than my body. I am even more than my body and my mind. My soul existed before my body and it will exist after my body is gone. I learned this spiritual lesson that Tuesday in August sixteen years ago without even realizing it. But this was an important piece of the spiritual puzzle for me. This, in fact, is the foundation for my entire spiritual truth.

****

When I applied to USM, I had to define what spirituality means to me. Based on my experience with my mom's death, I wrote that I believe we are all spirits having a human experience. But even having this belief, it is still hard for me to experience it sometimes. During peak experiences, such as witnessing my mom's death, and giving birth to my two children, I have a knowingness in my body that I am more than a collection of cells. I can feel this truth clearly – how my physical body acts as an anchor for my spirit, which extends out around me and connects to everything else in the world. In ordinary times, I feel this most often in nature, when I'm doing something really fun and challenging that requires my focus and attention, and when I am at my best professionally, whether it is leading a workshop or having a meaningful conversation or guiding a healing session. More often in the daily rush of life, I have to remind myself that I'm not just a body doing stuff but that I really have a spirit . . . that I actually <u>am</u> a spirit. In addition to making my Dr. Doolittle dream come true, I hoped to gain from my experience at USM a deeper experience of spirit and connectedness. And I wanted that experience to happen more often. I was looking for the feeling of communion I had when I was a kid – that knowingness before words, that deep understanding that we are all one.

My first year at USM was a time to clear the emotional and mental debris that clouded my ability to connect with that spiritual part of me. In USM terms, I was learning how to recognize and express my authentic self. I healed old emotional wounds, cleared unconscious beliefs that had been holding me back from full self-expression, and I reclaimed my natural psychic abilities, abilities that today feel like part of my basic genetic make-up.

As I did all this personal healing work, my connection to and love for animals grew stronger in my awareness. Many childhood memories involved animals, both wild animals and family pets, that I had known or seen or dreamed about. My days as a scientist on research boats searching for or watching dolphins took on a new importance to me, too. And I felt the accumulated experience of every hour I had spent observing dolphins and seals and whales and manatees and birds and fish and otters and lizards. All the hours I had shared with animals seemed to be coalescing to a deeper understanding of how we all fit together.

Then, one day in class I had an epiphany and I just had to share it with the whole class. I stood up. My hand shook as I held the microphone close to my mouth to address my two teachers and my two hundred and seventy classmates in the large classroom. I took a deep breath, hoping to calm the butterflies inside me, and scanned the room, looking into the eyes of my classmates, many of whom I had worked with in class. I thanked them for giving me the ultimate gift, the gift of myself, the gift of helping me realize my spiritual truth. And then I told them how I see the two parts of my truth fitting together.

The first part of my spiritual truth is the conclusion that I reached after my mom's death that I'm not a human being who has occasional spiritual experiences, but that I am a spiritual being having a human experience. I think we're all here to learn spiritual lessons and each of us has a unique gift to offer the world. Our joys are our gifts and our challenges are our lessons. As a dramatic example, I think of all the rock stars who made amazing music and touched so many lives (their gifts) but were tortured by depression or insecurity (their lessons) and drank themselves to death or overdosed on drugs or even killed themselves. This is the foundation that leads to my second realization.

Secondly, I believe that all beings, humans and animals alike, are spiritual beings. It's my contention that, like humans, animals have a soul. Like us, they are also spirits having unique experiences that include spiritual lessons and gifts. They are here to have particular experiences that will help their soul to grow and evolve, experiences that they couldn't get any other way than being that particular kind of animal. I see humans and animals as equal, as the same, as being here for the same reasons.

There I said it, I thought to myself as I sat down. Simple, clear, honest. This is how I see the world. This is how I've always seen the world. This is simply a more detailed explanation of my childhood sense that we are all one, that we are all connected. It felt great to put my truth into words and to say those words out loud to almost 300 people. I was still shaking, my stomach was still in knots, but a warmth spread through my body, a confidence born of speaking my truth. I didn't care if anyone believed me or agreed with me or shared my truth. I had recognized my truth and that was what mattered to me most.

Testing My Spiritual Truth

Asking a Question, Creating a Hypothesis

For most of my adult life, I have felt like I've been ping ponging between two distinct selves: the scientific researcher and spiritual seeker. My psychic experiences happened mainly during those times that I was between science gigs (between college and master's degree and between master's and PhD) or with a circle of friends that was completely separate from and unrelated to my academic or scientific friends. I was in two different worlds that never met.

For years I wondered if both parts of me could exist simultaneously. I yearned to integrate both aspects of my being – I didn't want to have to lose or shut off one part of me in order to experience the other anymore. I wanted to be a renaissance woman, with a wide variety of aspects of myself expressed at the same time. That was how I decided that my second year project at USM (the University of Santa Monica) was going to be integrating my scientific and spiritual selves.

Over a period of several months, from the middle of my first year at USM to the early class weekends of the second year, I got wisps of inspiration for my second year project. In May, with my second year project heavy on my mind, I created a dream drawing for my future. As usual, I approached the process as a blank slate, with no expectations or ideas about what might show up. I closed my eyes, connected to my spirit and waited for inspiration to appear. After a few minutes, I saw in my mind's eye an image of a photograph of a dolphin named Delphi that I used to work with at Marine World. In the photo, he is smiling with his mouth open about to bite a bright yellow ball floating on the surface of his pool. I saw this photo taking up the bottom half of my drawing, but the top half was blank. I knew my first step and I recreated the photo of Delphi as best I could. When I had finished, I gazed at my drawing, remembering Delphi and his mischievous personality. A smile curled my lips and then a flood of words streamed into my consciousness: truth, love, guides, animal minds, consciousness, soul, puzzle pieces . . . and on and on the words came into my mind. I wrote them down on the blank upper half of my drawing at different angles and in different fonts in a random jumble of words and patterns. My take home message from this experience was this: once I connect to animals, the words will come to me. This was my first inkling that I would talk to animals and write a book. This experience has turned out to be prophetic because that's exactly what I've done for this book. I've connected with animals, all different kinds of animals, and their messages have flown to me, coming to me in great waves of feelings and words and pictures.

Last fall, as I started talking and listening to animals that I encountered - my friend's dog Molly, a snake in the park, dogs barking in a yard, I experienced my spiritual truth over and over again — I realized that they had more awareness, more consciousness, than a strictly biological perspective could account for. They had souls. Just as I was a divine being having my unique human experience, they were divine beings having their unique animal experiences. Like the dolphin I swam with in the Bahamas, these animals were no different from me fundamentally. I had a soul. They had a soul. We were the same beings in different skins. This was my spiritual truth. It felt right to me; it felt true to me; but I realized that my spiritual truth was still untested, it was just an idea that I had. I felt in my heart that animals are spiritual beings but why not find out? I turned my spiritual truth into a hypothesis. For my second year project I would test a spiritual question with scientific methods. My scientific and spiritual selves were integrating nicely.

Most of the science I have done has been behavioral observations. For my master's thesis, I recorded the behavior and relative positions of captive bottlenose dolphins calves and their moms from the time the babies were born until their first birthdays. For my PhD dissertation, I boated through my research area looking for dolphins. When I found them, I recorded similar data: the behavior of a group of dolphins, their group size, their location, the depth of the water, the weather conditions, and time of day of the sighting. I took a photograph of the dorsal fin of as many dolphins as I could to create a photo library of all the individuals I could identify. Then I compiled all the information for each sighting and for each dolphin and examined the patterns that emerged.

I've also conducted scientific experiments. At the California Academy of Sciences, I co-led a research project with another graduate student studying the effects of environmental enrichment for captive Pacific white-sided dolphins and harbor seals. Three times a week for several months, we would lower a xylophone-looking contraption over the pool wall that held two dolphins and three seals. When one of the marine mammals pushed a "key" (one of the PVC tubes that hung into the water), something would happen. All the animals would either get fed or get a chance to play in a hose of water sprayed into the pool or music (James Taylor for one key and classical for another key) played through underwater speakers. They could also choose to listen to vocalizations of wild dolphins. We found that the food key was the most popular activity and James Taylor was the most often requested acoustical selection.

As a PhD student, I participated in more "classical" scientific experiments with other animal species, studying the foraging behavior of ground squirrels, the genetic relationships of different populations of an endangered desert fish called the tui chub, and the effects of different diets on chuckwallas (medium-sized desert lizards). The chuckwallas were divided into two groups; one group received a high quality diet (high in nutrients and low in dietary fiber) and the other received a low quality diet (more dietary fiber than nutrients). Each lizard was weighed before and after feeding and we tested their resting metabolism before and after the treatment phase of the experiment, the time that we fed them the special diets. In this case, the diet differences didn't affect their metabolism or their temperature regulating behavior as we expected it might.

So, I've had experience with several different ways to conduct scientific investigations but none of my experiences would help me here. Behavioral observations would not help me answer my question. Experiments weren't possible and even if they were, they would not be effective methods to test my hypothesis. So, I turned to a method used more often in sociology and psychology: case studies. My approach is to present ten different case studies, one for each species, that together will illustrate the results of my inquiry into the nature of spirit. This is an approach that has a long history in many fields and it can yield information and insights unobtainable in other ways.

All science begins with a question. What do you want to find out about? What are you curious about? Scientists ask their questions and then rearrange them in the format of a testable statement called a hypothesis. My hypothesis is my spiritual truth: animals are spiritual beings with their unique curriculum (spiritual learning) and gifts (service to the planet). To test this hypothesis, I used my intuitive communication skills to interview individuals from ten species of animals. I asked each animal the same three questions: What is your spiritual lesson? What is your spiritual gift? Do you have a message you want to share with humans?

Format of this Book

Each of the upcoming chapters focuses on one animal species. For a foundational understanding of each animal, I examine the symbolism of the animals in mythology and worldwide spiritual traditions and relate the most interesting and relevant aspects of their natural history. Then I present the results of my spiritual research and share the animals' responses to my three questions: What is your spiritual lesson? What is your spiritual gift? What message do you have for humans?

Ever since I was a little girl swimming in Lake Michigan pretending to be a seal, I've always imagined what reality was like for other animals. What does it feel like to fly in a flock of birds? To swim in a school of fish? To slither along the hot sand of a desert? When I was a research assistant studying wild dolphins in Texas, I would swim in Matagorda Bay on my days off. Swim fins on my feet and mask and snorkel on my face, I would slap the water with my "tail" as I'd seen the dolphins do. Scientists thought that tail slaps were a sign of anger or displeasure. I wanted to see how it felt in my body to do that. Would I feel powerful and angry or playful and coquettish? My experience was inconclusive – I felt a little of both. During the writing of this book I discovered that I have the ability to energetically bring my awareness into the form of any animal and feel in my body what it feels like to be that animal, whether it be an alligator or a giraffe or a cat. So, each chapter of Divine Beings includes my experience of what it feels like to be each animal.

The chapters are arranged in the order that I encountered each animal on my journey through the year that I spent researching and writing this book. I begin with dogs because that is where my love of animals began and where my intuitive breakthrough occurred, with my friend Ellery's dog, Bear. I work my way through all the other species and share the insights and shifts in my consciousness that occurred along the way.

Finally, in the last chapter of this book, I tie my whole journey together and answer the question: "What does it all mean?" Embracing or adopting the spiritual paradigm that every being is a divine being, other shifts can occur in your life. What are the choices that we can make in our lives to honor this new understanding and get the most out of it? This chapter is a call to action to the reader, an invitation to each of us to live our truth, to allow all of our actions and words to be guided by our inner knowing, our spiritual truths.

Part Two: Messages from the Animals

DOGS, Canis lupus familiaris

My love affair with dogs began when I was very young. For my third Christmas, I received a larger-than-life-sized stuffed dog named "Cuddly Dudley." Golden tan and at least a foot taller than me, Dudley was the love of my young life. When I was old enough to get my own real dog, around age 14, I named my fluffy white female Samoyed puppy "Dudley" (and got a lot of puzzled looks from adults that we encountered on our walks).

I loved my new Dudley even more than I loved my first Dudley. I took Dudley to obedience classes and for walks through our neighborhood each night. After my parents divorced, Dudley and I used to explore the marshes and saltwater creeks near my mom's house in northern California for hours, lost in our own worlds together. Dudley had a fox-like way of pouncing over the tall marsh grass as she tried to capture small animals. I never saw her catch anything, but I can still picture her above the green grass, her white paws hanging close to each other in the air as her back arched toward the sky, her black eyes intent on the ground below her. After our adventures, we would traipse back up the hill to home, trailing black prints of marsh tar behind us. By the time we entered my mom's house our feet would be clean.

When I entered high school a few years later, Dudley started wandering away from my mom's new home in the "flats" of our town. One night she wandered away and never returned. I felt so alone and lost without her but I also felt bad that the turmoil in our human lives might have spilled over into her and I secretly thought she was looking for a more peaceful place to live. I hope she found that.

I waited fifteen long years before bringing another dog into my life. After graduating from college, I spent most of my twenties traveling through the United States and Costa Rica as a whitewater rafting guide when I wasn't a graduate student in San Francisco and Reno. Some of my fellow guides had dogs that lived with them, but I always felt that I wanted to have more stability in my life before bringing a pet into it. My boyfriend, Chris (now my husband), and I bought a house together in Florida after he completed his MBA and after I finished collecting data for my PhD dissertation. Before our house went into escrow, I was looking for a dog. We found a beautiful little ball of Australian shepherd fluff that we brought home the week after we moved in. She was unique and quirky. While her littermates were rolling all over each other being clumsy and silly, she was wandering off by herself very seriously exploring the cattle farm that was her birth home in northern Tampa. A black tri (mostly black with bits of brown and patches of white on her chest and feet), she was almost named Sierra or Echo. But she was a unique dog who needed a unique name, and we already knew other dogs with those names. Then one day as I was driving in the car the Grateful Dead cover of an old Cajun song came on the radio and "Iko" got her name.

Iko was my constant companion as I analyzed my data and wrote my dissertation chapters. She was usually at my feet when I was at the computer and she forced me to take breaks and play outside at regular intervals. I am grateful for both influences. One afternoon, we were sitting out on the grass in our backyard. I'd been reading the book "What the Animals Tell Me" by Sonia Fitzpatrick and decided to try out one of the suggested exercises with Iko. I sent Iko the thought, "If you walk inside the house right now, I'll give you a treat." To my great surprise, she lifted her head, gave me a puzzled look of "Really? That's all I have to do?" and got up and walked through her dog door into the house. Of course I followed her and gave her a treat. This was my first experience with intuitive communication with an animal that was verifiable and objectively successful. It would take me another ten years, and a conversation with Bear, to know that the communication could go both ways. I am forever grateful to Iko for so many things, but right now I'm especially grateful for that glimmer of hope that she gave me that afternoon that somehow intuitive communication with animals really was possible for me.

I'm not the only one to have great love for my dog companions. There are about 77.5 million other dog owners in the United States today and in 2001, there were an estimated 400 million dogs in the world. The first animal to be domesticated (roughly 15,000 years ago), dogs have been the most widely kept working, hunting, and companion animal in human history. They have been selectively bred to help humans with hunting, herding, protection, and police and military assistance. More recently, dogs of all species have been trained to help handicapped people with everything from opening doors to navigating traffic to predicting seizures.

When I began my quest to learn about the spiritual realities of animals, many friends asked if I would need to talk to more than one individual of each species in order to get a full understanding of each animal's spiritual truth. It's a good question. Like humans, each individual animal is unique; each has his or her own perspective on life and his or her own take on my questions. But the answers that dogs gave to my three questions were remarkably similar. I'll illustrate this with answers from three different dogs living in different situations with their people.

The first dog I asked, a one-year old Rhodesian ridgeback named Layla, told me that her spiritual gift was love and devotion. Her ability to give and receive love and devotion was her special gift. She loved and was devoted to her owner, Edie, and her boyfriend, Jeff, and his three children that stayed with them regularly. She felt that she offered Edie a special opportunity, the opportunity to give love and devotion to her that as a childless woman, Edie wouldn't have any other way. Layla said her spiritual lesson was feeling deep emotions physically in her body and feeling alone when her humans weren't with her. Layla's message to humans had a lot of exclamation points. This is the way she answered my question: "Get dirty! Play! Have fun! And give and receive love unconditionally."

The next dog that I talked to and asked my questions to was Maddie, my classmate Angela's dog. Maddie said that her spiritual gift was to teach Angela that love lasts. She is teaching her this by giving her the direct experience of it happening. Maddie, a rescue dog who had lived in two other homes before settling in with Angela, said that her spiritual lesson was also that love lasts. This is something she is learning through her experience of having Angela stick by her and love her and having it be for good. She is teaching this to Angela and she is learning it herself. I didn't ask Maddie if she had a message for people, but she did have a message for Angela's father who watches her when Angela is out of town for work. She said, "Tell Pop-Pop that he is the light of my life."

Finally, I asked my three questions to Molly, a standard poodle living with a family, who told me that her spiritual gift was enthusiastic love. She said, "I am a source of love, unconditional love that can be given out to you and you can receive it. My love is like a balm for the scraped parts of your soul. I am here to love you all [my family] no matter what." Molly said that her spiritual lesson was to grow in wisdom through understanding the loving bonds between beings, learning about love in all different kinds of ways, experiencing the joy of love and the pain of disconnection. She told me that that's what gives her wisdom. She said that she does that by "learning from the love we share and seeing the rifts between my people, seeing it unfold in front of my eyes and loving everyone through it." When I asked her what her human family can learn from her, she responded, "That loves lasts. That love is constant. That love softens the blows and even heals. Tell them to let it go, don't hang on to the hurts, and play." Molly said that her message to humans is "Remember to play and have fun and be silly. Silly is good. Don't take yourselves too seriously. Let's just play together and love together and it will all work out. Don't take us for granted. We are here for ourselves but we are also here for you. Because you don't hear us speaking to you, sometimes you don't see us, but we are still here and we are aware and present. Your kindness means a lot to us. Please be gentle and kind and know that it is appreciated and noticed."

I love how the different personalities of all the dogs come through in their responses to my three questions. But these three examples were remarkably similar, too. As you'll see as you read the responses from other species of animals in this book, not every animal is about giving and receiving love. I was particularly struck by the fact that two dogs mentioned that their lesson was that "love lasts." During my readings with dogs that are about to die, they often tell me that they will return and visit their owners in a non-physical form. They even tell me how their owners will be able to recognize that they are there, usually with a nuzzle on the cheek or a cold nose pressed against a hand. Some tell me that they will come back as another pet to live with their owners again. Love, indeed, does last and last and last with dogs.

I know my love for Dudley hasn't diminished over the thirty-plus years that I have lived without her, and my love for Iko will go on forever, too. I tell my kids that Iko is my "first baby" and they understand that I love her as if she were one of my children. She is part of me and part of my family. She has given me the opportunity to give and receive love unconditionally, to take care of someone with no chance of ever asking for anything in return. But she does give me something in addition to the opportunity to love and care for her, she loves me fully every day of her life. To be the recipient of that kind of unconditional love is a deep, profound, joyful experience.

When I think about what spiritual opportunities dogs offer us, I'm reminded of the old story about the wandering monks who owned no possessions except for the saffron robes they wore on their backs and the bowl and spoon they carried with them for eating. They never knew when their next meal would come and they would knock on doors and "beg" for food. This wasn't selfish. Sure, it served a purpose for them, to give them food for survival, but their habit of begging for food provided the people of that region an opportunity to be generous, an opportunity that they might not have had if the monks hadn't showed up at their doorsteps that day. In giving we receive and dogs give us our opportunity to give unconditional love which is a gift that we might otherwise miss. And they give it to us day after day after day.

Talking to dogs has become a regular occurrence for me now. When I stay at my friend Debra's house when I'm in Los Angeles, I always have at least one conversation with her dog Molly. On the Saturday morning of the first USM weekend of the Second Year, soon after my first conversation with Ellery's dog Bear, Eric and Debra were still asleep as I crept quietly back into their house after an early morning jog through their neighborhood. Molly greeted me with her tail wagging and eyes shining. "Good morning, Molly! How are you?" I asked out loud. I didn't get an intuitive response, but she wagged her whole body vigorously and smiled up at me. "Did you have any dreams last night?" I asked, more to be polite than really expecting a response. But I immediately saw a clear picture of Molly in my mind's eye. She was chasing squirrels around and up a tree. "Really?" I asked her. "Anything else?" In the next picture I saw, she was on a beautiful tropical beach with a long, wide expanse of white sand unfolding between palm trees swaying in the breeze and a crystal clear, turquoise ocean that was worthy of a Corona beer commercial. In the middle of the beach was Molly, in heaven as she scratched her back in the sand, her spine snaking through the sand and her paws digging at the sky. Not another soul was in sight and Molly was in rapture. A huge smile lit up my face – what a perfect dream for a dog! I loved that she had a dream and that she shared it with me. When I told Debra and Eric about it, Eric commented that Molly does love to roll on her back to scratch it.

"Talking" to Molly about her dream reminded me that dogs have their own reality. They have their own awareness and their own dreams. Their wiring is really similar to ours and it suddenly made sense to me that she would have a dream like that – all that sand would be a limitless opportunity to do something that she did all the time in her normal waking hours that felt really good to her. I stay with Eric and Debra a few times a year and each time a layer of richness is added to my life through my growing relationship with Molly. She is showing me pieces of her life that give me insights into the lives of all dogs.

Spiritually, dogs generally symbolize faithfulness, protection, loyalty, and service to humanity. This is one case where the animals have been portrayed pretty accurately and congruently with who they are and why they say they are here. As you'll soon see, however, this isn't always the case.

AFRICAN ELEPHANT, *Loxodonta Africana*

As a child born in the sixties, I, like many of my contemporaries, grew up reading books about Babar the kind-hearted elephant king created by Laurent de Brunhoff and Horton the equally kind-hearted elephant created by Dr. Seuss. Like most elephants in children's books, these two characters were portrayed as models of exemplary behavior. Although Walt Disney's Dumbo was cast in a similar light, I could never relate to him (except to envy his ability to fly) and, to be totally honest, he kind of creeped me out. My allegiances lay with Babar and Horton.

Babar, the anthropomorphic elephant king, was a noble hero with many desirable human qualities. He was sweet, tender, courageous, merciful, thoughtful and wise. I lost myself in his utopic kingdom and was particularly intrigued by his monkey sidekick and the relationship between the two friends of different species. They each seemed to display their unique personality traits (what scientists call their species-specific behaviors) as strengths while honoring and respecting their limitations and differences. King Babar was a wise and just king who created a good country for all his subjects to live in, regardless of species.

Horton was another elephant character whose concern for others in his community was depicted as a model to emulate. First, he saved the microscopic Whos in microscopic Whoville in spite of disruption and derision by his jungle contemporaries. Then, in the second book in the series, he agreed to hatch an egg for a flighty bird who preferred travel and leisure to being tied down by motherhood. Even in the face of boredom, bad weather, teasing from his friends, and elephant hunters, Horton stayed on the nest with the egg for a year because, in his own words, "I meant what I said and I said what I meant . . . an elephant's faithful one hundred percent!"

My first glimpse of an elephant in real life most likely occurred at the Brookfield Zoo outside of Chicago when I was a small child, but I have no memory of that. The first elephant I remember seeing was at the San Francisco Zoo. I was in third grade and my family had recently moved to California from Illinois. My three siblings and I spent an entire day exploring Golden Gate Park and the Zoo with our father.

It was a brisk fall day and the guardrail on the viewers' side of the concrete moat around the elephant yard was cold on my hands and my middle as I leaned against it, straining for a closer look. The adult female elephant on the other side was enormous and powerful-looking. She must have been very strong because she had a manacle around one ankle that was attached to a chain not much longer than she was. The other end was fastened to a post in the ground. It seemed a sad existence to me even at that young age. I thought it ironic that the zookeepers had installed a shower in her yard for her to use whenever she desired. All she had to do was use her trunk to pull another, thinner chain that hung from the handle next to the showerhead suspended from the wall of the elephant house. Elephants like showers, the sign near the cold fence told us. To my young mind, it seemed a small consolation for an animal restricted to a circle of ground less than two body lengths in diameter to be able to take a shower whenever she wanted. Especially in San Francisco where, as Mark Twain famously said, "The coldest winter I ever spent was a summer in San Francisco." Brrrrr. An elephant shower in San Francisco could make a lot of goose bumps!

As a graduate student at San Francisco State University years later, I would visit her again, this time behind the scenes with a zookeeper guide, my "Zoo Biology" classmates, and our instructor, Hal Markowitz, who conducted environmental enrichment research at the zoo. My thoughts and feelings about captive elephants were unchanged from when I was in third grade, but now I had lots of scientific information to support my gut feelings.

Penny, the San Francisco Zoo elephant, was an African bush elephant, one of the three species of elephants recognized by scientists today. (The other two are the African forest elephant and the Asian elephant.) African bush elephants are the largest of the three species as well as the largest living land animal. Males are larger than females and they can be as tall (at the shoulders) as 13 feet but average closer to 12 feet. They can weigh as much as 12 tons (twenty-four *thousand* pounds). African elephants typically live for 50 to 70 years, which accounts for my ability to see Penny as an eight year old third grader and as a twenty-three year old graduate student. The longest elephant life ever recorded is 82 years.

Although a lion may occasionally take down a very small or sick young elephant, adult elephants have no known natural predators. Females live in tightly knit matriarchal societies, while males are mainly solitary as adults. New research, however, is documenting socially complex bachelor herds that congregate predictably in specific locations and at specific times of the year.

Herbivores that can move widely throughout their large ranges, elephants communicate over long distances (up to six miles) using ultrasonic (low frequency) sounds that may travel through the ground itself. Elephants receive the sounds through the sensitive skin on the pads of their feet and their trunks, either lifting one foreleg off the ground or laying their trunks onto the ground for better reception.

In many Asian spiritual traditions, elephants symbolize royalty, fertility and wisdom. I can totally understand this symbolism. Elephants have an imperious bearing, most likely due to the confidence born of a life with no threats from predators. They are large, robust and healthy-looking, sure signs of fertility. And their great heads advertise similarly large brains. Ganesha, the Hindu god of wisdom, is represented as having the body of a man (often with several pairs of arms) and the head of an elephant. Sometimes known as the Remover of Obstacles, Ganesha is also said to be the patron of arts and literature and the god of the intellect. Elephants, as they plow through a forest uprooting trees taller than themselves, might also be considered "removers of obstacles." They surely let nothing stand in their way. In our modern American culture, elephants are also famed for their memory -- as evidenced by the common phrase "An elephant never forgets" -- and their intelligence, which scientists rank at equal to that of dolphins and primates. The great thinker Aristotle once admired the elephant as "the beast which passeth all others in wit and mind."

At the San Diego Zoo in January, I intuitively spoke to an African bull elephant and asked him my three questions. He responded that the spiritual gift of elephants is honoring ancestors and maintaining the traditions and the wisdom of their lineage. They are record keepers who keep the ancient flames of wisdom alive in their daily decisions and actions. Their spiritual challenges are keeping the old ways alive in the face of global change and integrating new information and situations with the older traditions. It is a challenge for them to honor the old and honor the new. Their biggest challenge is to stay open and fresh and present in the moment to what is happening. My impression was that elephants would rather that everything stayed roughly the same forever so that adapting to new circumstances would never be required of them.

The bull elephant's message to humans is "we need to be ourselves to be healthy and to live our true path, our way. There is no compromise. We need to have room and space and food to be ourselves and to live our true path and our way. These are basic needs. They must be met. These are not optional."

These responses are echoed in the messages of an elephant I met early in my journey. On the same day that I first talked to Bear and found out why she was mad at Kale, another astonishing thing happened, another intuitive milestone for me that forever after became known as the "Angry Elephant Incident." Ellery and I were sitting at her table talking and catching up when she suddenly said that there was an African elephant spirit in the room. "Yeah, right," I thought to myself. "How could that happen?" But then I could see her, too, just to the left of me, between the table and the kitchen door.

"Talk to her, Cara. She's here to talk to you."

"But she's really angry!" I protested. This was too much. I'd already spontaneously talked to her dog, and now I was supposed to talk to angry elephant spirits that just showed up out of the blue?! What was this world coming to?!

Ellery just gave me a patient look. Her bemused smile comforted me and reminded me that I could do this. There was just no slacking around Ellery. So, I consciously centered myself, opened myself to be receptive, and sent a tentative greeting to the elephant. I immediately received an intuitive message from her, an image of her stomping on huts, mad at the people living in them for invading her land and getting in her way.

I asked her why she was here and she said she had a message for people. The Angry Elephant showed me that each female elephant carried all the knowledge and experiences of her ancestors and her lineage in her awareness. She showed me how the Elephant Graveyards were an opportunity for an elephant to connect energetically with the experiences of other elephants not in her lineage. I saw how the big, soft pads of the elephants' feet were sensitive energy receivers for picking up memories from the life of the elephant whose bones she touched. The Bone Yards were important for elephants in order for them to stay connected with everyone, especially elephants not in their matriarchal lineage. The only way the Angry Elephant had access to the wisdom and experience of elephants in other matrilines was through contact with their bones in the Bone Yards. The Bone Yards act as a touchstone for elephants with both their past and with their more distant relatives and ancestors.

The Angry Elephant then showed me an image of the long view of an elephant's life. It looked like a spiral looping endlessly from the past into the future. Each loop represented the life of a single elephant; the whole spiral was a matriarchal lineage. All the lives were connected and incorporated in the loop. Each life honored the traditions of one generation passed on to the next. This elephant spirit felt like humans were getting in the way of her living out her traditions. And she was pissed!

I sent my questions as words to the Angry Elephant and in return I received images and impressions for at least ten minutes. The images were clear and powerful and they were layered with so much information and emotion that the experience became physically intense for me. Soon my head was spinning and I couldn't keep up with the barrage of what I've come to call feeling-pictures, images overlaid with layers of strong emotions on top of more layers of information. I had no filter, so I felt all the elephant's emotions in my body, albeit less intensely than if they were my own. Luckily, just when I was about to become too overwhelmed, the elephant felt her message had been received and she gently faded away from our awareness. It took me two to three times as long to explain my impressions to Ellery as it had to receive them because they were so rich in information and experience.

Both the African bull elephant at the San Diego Zoo and the Angry Elephant spirit that visited me in Ellery's house have similar serious messages for humans. As a species, African elephants are in grave danger of extinction. At the turn of the 20th century, there were an estimated 5 to 10 million of them, but hunting and habitat destruction reduced their numbers to less than half a million by the dawn of the 21st century. National Parks in Africa are the elephants' last hope for survival but these are not foolproof. Elephants often range through larger areas than are contained within parks. If they are restricted from traditional winter feeding grounds or spring breeding areas, many may die. If they are fenced in, they may destroy the very area designed to save them through overcrowding ranges that are too small to sustain the ecological impact of so many large, powerful mammals.

The plight of the elephants and the pleas (well, more like demands) from the two elephants I communicated with remind me that our modern cultures do less well with reality than they do with technology. The ancient humans knew elephants, the real elephants. They recognized their intelligence, devotion to ancestors and tradition, and honored the unique size, stature, and strength of elephants. Even the children's book authors who were my early influences in all things elephant recognized in them many of the best qualities of human beings. Horton' refrain "An elephant is faithful one hundred percent" takes on a new meaning for me now. Elephants are faithful to their families, their ancestors and their traditions. And they need to be able to continue to do that in order to survive.

With each species that we lose from the planet, we lose a piece of ourselves as well. If we lose elephants, we lose an even bigger piece of ourselves than we do with other species. Elephants have excited our hearts, minds and souls for untold generations. Their history is intertwined with ours. If we lose them, we lose a piece of our souls. We can use our technology and our minds to help save them, but the effort has to be directed by our hearts and souls. The impulse must come from the very essence of who we are and what we share with elephants in order for there to be a lasting solution. We must begin by looking into their eyes and seeing their souls. From there, our shared truth will become clear and we can move forward in a way that honors their needs and ours. We can find a common ground and build on it. Let's make that happen as soon as we can.

HORSE, Equus ferus

After my parents divorced, my dad moved to a small, rural town along the coast of northern California. Just a block from his house was a horse stable and on our way to the ocean, we would walk by it and sometimes we would stop and watch young riders learning the fine art of horseback riding. This was my only exposure to horses and riding up to this point. All that I knew about horses I had learned from watching "Mr. Ed" on black and white television after school. As far as I could tell, horses were wise, knowledgeable and sarcastic, while humans (as modeled by Wilbur, Mr. Ed's goofy owner) were dense, always getting into trouble, and incapable of taking care of themselves.

It was perhaps inevitable that in my dad's small town I would meet someone who would own a horse and invite me to go for a ride on one. My chance came when I was a freshman in high school. It was a hot summer day and I wore only a pair of cut off shorts and a tank top. We rode bareback along the trails that meandered through eucalyptus groves and within minutes my thighs were covered in hives and my eyes were itchy and watering.

Even after I discovered my allergy, I was still intrigued by and attracted to horses, but I generally loved them from afar. In high school, my mom and I did a horse camping trip in the national park area of our home. The two of us and our guide rode our horses (I was wearing long blue jeans and a long sleeve shirt) up into the dry, brown summer grasslands of Marin County and through the Blue Oak woodlands dotting the hillsides. We spent a warm summer night camping and returned the next morning to our home. It was a lovely, rare experience to be camping alone with my mom and I still savor the memory today.

I had one more interaction with horses between that camping trip and the beginning of this book. My friend and PhD classmate Erik invited me visit the University's horses with him one warm afternoon. Thinking I might have outgrown my allergy, I brought carrots and apples and immediately started stroking noses and brushing manes. Within minutes I could barely see through my swollen eyes and I rushed to the bathroom to rinse any remnants of horse from my eyes and mouth, which was starting to feel funny, too. I waited by the car, as far from the horses as I could be and still see them, as Erik made his rounds, visiting with each of his four-legged friends.

Fifteen years later, Ellery and I took our first field trip two weeks after my fateful conversation with her dog Bear. We went to visit some horses that Ellery worked with occasionally at a ranch on the outskirts of town. All of the horses were rescue horses, taken care of with love and devotion by a couple in their mid-fifties. The hills to the east were tan and green, just like the hills of my earlier campout with my mom. Something was bothering Fred, one of the eight horses living there, but the owner, Alice, didn't know the cause and she didn't tell us what part of his body was bothering him. We were on our own to figure it out.

We parked in a wide dirt driveway between the house and the yard on a windy afternoon. I dosed myself with a homeopathic remedy for animal dander allergies, grounded myself, and stepped out of my car. I knew nothing about any of the horses, only that one was named Fred and he had something wrong with him. Butterflies tickled my stomach but I remained calm and self-assured on the outside (I hoped!). I was curious to see what would happen. This was the first time I was going to "talk" to an animal on purpose and the tension was rising in my body in anticipation.

We walked through the bright yard past the white clapboard house on our left and the exercise rings on our right and into the shadows of the barn. Five horses were in their stalls here and we crossed straight over to Fred. Immediately an image flashed into my mind of a tired old cowboy slumped on a bench in front of a barn. He looked about a hundred years old, but he still radiated an air of confident swagger and wiry strength. I told Ellery what I saw and she laughed, explaining to me that Fred was a retired rodeo horse who had performed in every rodeo event there was. As we watched him from the stall gate, Fred ambled past us, showing off his bod. I sensed that he was a real charmer, like Rhett Butler, a lady's man, a tough guy with a heart. He was very sweet and seemed to want to sweep me off my feet and make me fall in love with him. It worked.

But we were here to do a job and I closed my eyes and put a picture of his body up on a screen in my mind's eye. Nothing stood out right away, so I started doing a scan from his tail toward his head. When I got to his head, the space between his ears lit up like a warning light. I mentioned my finding to Ellery who was silently doing similar work next to me. She felt the problem was in his left ear – we were in synch. A memory popped into my head of my master's degree adviser whom I hadn't spoken to in almost two decades. Dr. Hal Markowitz had been on a research trip in Costa Rica over the summer and in the fall of my second year he suddenly started having excruciating pain in the back of his head. It turned out that while he was camping in the rainforest, a bot fly had laid eggs under the skin of his neck and they were now hatched and eating their way through his head. His intense pain was caused by them chomping on his nerves.

Because this was such an odd memory to surface now I paid attention to it. Then I remembered that my teachers had taught us that intuition works through the person doing the work. My intuition had triggered this memory to give me the information that Fred's problem might be caused by a bot fly. Trepidatiously, I mentioned my memory to Ellery. "Trepidatiously" because for all I knew bot flies were an exotic species of flies that live only in Costa Rica. It seemed likely since the only time I had ever heard of bot flies was from Hal and his experience.

Ellery agreed with me that Fred's problem might be a bot fly. As we watched him, we noticed that he would shake his head every once in a while, kind of like a swimmer trying to get water out of his ear. As we talked and watched Fred, we developed a theory: we thought that a bot fly (or some other kind of fly) had walked into Fred's left ear and laid some eggs that were bothering him either in egg form or as new hatchlings that were causing him discomfort. It all made sense to us.

We asked Fred if we could help him and he said yes. When we asked if Ellery could take the flies or eggs out of his ear, he said, "No!" Ellery heard him repeating, "Alice – the vet. Alice – the vet." And we knew he didn't trust us with such a delicate operation but he knew that Alice could call the vet whom he would trust with his sensitive ear.

We shared all this with Alice and she immediately took her cell phone into the yard, called the vet, and made an appointment for a visit the next day. When we asked Alice about bot flies (and told her the story of Hal's experience), she said that bot flies do live in northern California. In fact, she picks them off the horses' legs all the time, but, according to her, "they can't get in horses' ears." I didn't argue with her – who really cares what species it was or if it's possible for bot flies to get into horses' ears? The point was that we figured out Fred's problem and helped him with it. Ellery and I both did an energy healing on Fred to help him feel more comfortable until the vet arrived the next day.

Alice asked us to ask Fred if he wanted to retire completely and just rest. His answer was a vehement "no!" He loved walking around with Alice's granddaughter Sierra on his back, even if he had to rest and recover for two days after each jaunt. He loved Sierra and he loved making her happy.

After talking to Fred's neighbor, Hollywood, an orange cat, and three barking dogs, as well as Alice and Dan the human caretakers, we loaded back in to my car to head home, tired but happy. We'd spent almost three hours at the ranch, most of it doing intuitive work, which demands focus and stamina and is something to train your body to handle slowly over time. It can really wear you out. I had jumped right into the deep end of the psychic pool! But I came up swimming. My victory that day was connecting deeply with an individual who happened to be a horse. I had made a new friend and I had helped him with a problem that had been bothering him for several weeks. All in all, this was an amazing first field trip for me. I got lots of good, clear, helpful information from talking to the horses. It was actually easy to talk to them. I was surprised that I got pictures and feelings and impressions and memories but no words. But I wasn't going to quibble about that! I was on Cloud 9! I did it! It was easy and natural for me! What a world!

As I drove home, contented and just a little bit itchy in the eyes, I commented to Ellery, "Horses seem to have big hearts, like they are centered in their heart chakras." "Yep," she said knowingly, "they sure do."

Horses as we know them today evolved about 50 million years ago. Around 4,000 BC horses were domesticated and since then they have been used by humans in warfare, for farm work, for sport, for shows, and, more recently, for therapy. Przewalsky's horse is the only remaining truly wild horse that has never been domesticated in its history. These rare horses live in small, endangered groups in the wild. Feral horses, like those currently living in the open lands of California and Nevada, live in the wild but are descended from domesticated horses. Horses average a 25-30 year lifespan. They are prey animals with a strong flight instinct – when startled they tend to run away, not stay and fight.

In Native American traditions, horses represent travel, power and freedom. They are a symbol of sexual desire as well as a symbol of clairvoyance and the magical side of humans. The Norse god Odin is depicted on an eight-legged steed. In Chinese astrology, people born in the year of the Horse are said to be popular, cheerful, persuasive, perceptive, wise, and adventurous. They have freedom without restraint.

On a later visit, I asked my friend Fred my three questions. He told me that the spiritual gift of the horse is love, vitality, athleticism, movement, speed and partnership. The spiritual lesson for domesticated horses is dedication and devotion. They are here to learn how it feels to be powerful but dependent on someone else. As a domesticated animal the best outcome of this challenge is interdependence, when the horse and rider merge into one being. The message Fred wants to share with humans is that you have to open up the door to your heart in order to let someone else in. Doing it is your choice; you are in charge. Fred says, "I love my gifts and my people. I love making them smile. I love to light up their eyes and their faces. Open yourself up to the other's gift, whoever that other is. Be neighborly, invite them in. We can all give and receive in so many ways. I used to love to entertain and work hard together. Now I love to give smiles because that means someone has opened their door (heart) to me."

After talking to Fred, I decide to experience reality through a horse's senses. When I felt into how it feels to be a horse, the first thing that I noticed was how my awareness was centered in the heart center, which was large and powerful. Aha! Just as I had suspected since my first visit with Fred! I was right! I was sitting in a chair with my hands resting palms up on my thighs, but I felt the need to straighten my arms and turn them so my palms were facing my body. I turned my head from side to side, feeling how long my neck and face were and the power in my chest and legs. My head felt far from my body and a little bit separate. My legs felt spindly, like stilts on small feet. My body had an awkward sense of balance to me, like I might tip over at any moment, but I felt how two can become one when riding together – at its best. Merging of the two separate selves (horse and human) into one unit – I knew this was exciting, invigorating, joyful, fleeting and rare for horse and rider. I knew that this was the feeling that Fred had loved as a rodeo horse whether he was barrel racing or roping a calf. He loved that feeling of communion between him and his rider.

A month after my first visit, I went back to see Fred again. He had gotten sick and was having a hard time standing and seemed to be in pain. Alice's husband Dan had spent the night before sleeping in his stall, rising occasionally to make sure that Fred didn't lie in one position for too long and die. When I saw Fred

I gasped in shock – he looked so old and broken down, not at all the charismatic horse that I had met a few short weeks ago. He was standing along the wall in a funny way, with his head just above his water dish on the adjacent wall. His back looked more dipped to me and his hips looked funny and misshapen. I said, "Hi, Fred. How are you doing?" and he said, "I'm sad. I don't want to go away. I don't want to leave." I felt that he wanted to stay with Alice and Dan and their granddaughter Sierra and he didn't want to die. I assured him that we would do everything we could to help him get better so he could stay here.

I intuitively scanned his body and saw a triangle of pain and tightness along the top of his back from a single point at the middle of his shoulders back to a point on either hip. Ellery and I did energy work on him for over an hour. My attention kept being drawn to a point in his left rear abdomen. I asked my guides for help and clarification and nothing clearly came to me but I kept mulling over Fred's legs giving out on him, the triangle of pain and tightness along his back. It reminded me of how I felt when I'd had kidney stones the summer before. My back kept giving out on me and my legs would buckle and I'd fall over and have to catch myself before I hit the ground, excruciating pain radiating through my back. In fact, I'd been thinking about all these thing since we'd arrived but suddenly it occurred to me that Fred might have a kidney stone. The veterinarian's test showed no indication of kidney stones, but my experience with the bot fly memory was still fresh in my mind so I didn't take those as being conclusive. It was still a possibility, I thought.

We worked on Fred a little longer and he was gradually improving. He walked across his stall slowly but fairly smoothly. He held his head a little higher. He wasn't leaning against the wall anymore; he was able to support his weight with his own legs.

Fred is the only horse that I know in this kind of depth. For me, he is the paragon of all horses. He is kind, loving, generous, dedicated, charming, brave – I could go on and on about him. He embodies all the qualities the Chinese recognized when they created their zodiac system: he's popular, cheerful, persuasive, perceptive, wise, and adventurous. The Native Americans were right on the money, too. Fred helps his people to travel, he's powerful, and when he reaches that point of communion with his rider, he embodies a sense of freedom that transcends his domesticated existence. As a symbol of sexual desire, Fred shines, too. It's like the term "animal magnetism" was created to describe him. The Native Americans also thought of horses as symbols of clairvoyance and the magical side of humans. For me, that was one of Fred's greatest gifts. He helped me develop my clairvoyant abilities and see them in action with him. This process is truly magical and the connection possible between humans and animals on this level is truly enchanted. As an important personality on my journey, Fred will forever be in my heart. For his dear connection with his people, he will live on in their hearts forever.

OUR TELEPATHIC RIDE

"It's time now for silent journal writing"
That's what I thought he had said
But my mind took off to my white Appaloosa pony instead
I sent her a message; a quick how do you do?
But what I got back was: well where the heck are YOU?
And I tried to explain, as I had done before,
I had to be gone for just a day or two more.
But that doesn't mean that I'm too far away
To send you a hello, or a "how was your day"
I was just thinking of you and the ride that we'd had
Earlier this week, and it made me feel glad.
And as I smiled at her – she gave me a wink!
It seemed a little flirtatious, or so one might think.
But I responded right back and I blew her a kiss
Which she caught head on, and then asked me this:
Hey COWBOY would you like to go for a ride?
Without saddle or tack, just your legs by my side?
Come closer she said with a flick of her mane,
Which I happily obliged, my pretty white dame.
So I hopped on her back with no saddle or tack
And after a little walk we took off Without ever looking back!
Down the trail we went at a nice little trot
When we came to the road's fork –would we stop? Or would we not?
But we rounded the corner and flew up the hill
My hair and her mane flowing, Both loving our free will
And at the top of the hill we didn't slow down!
It was as if we were flying, never touching the ground
With the wind in our hair, and the sun on our face
We ran faster, and faster, till we came to the place
Where she had given me that wink, and I'd blown her that kiss
Where we met mind to mind and rode off in pure bliss
And I remember asking myself And asking her too
Was this YOUR dream about carrying me?
Or MY dream about me riding you?

-Bruce Harnishfeger, 3/29/11 USM class of 2011

GRAY WHALE, Eschrichtius robustus

Whales are large marine mammals that have captured humans' imaginations since time immemorial. The biblical story of Jonah and the whale symbolizes the resurrection and transformation that are possible by going within and surrendering to the ancient beast of your own making, your ego, so you can rebirth yourself through your own innate creativity. Native Americans regard whales as the Record Keepers of ancient knowledge and as symbols of creation and creativity. Living deep in a dark, cold, underwater world where sunlight cannot penetrate, whales communicate over the long, lonely distances through sound created in the huge resonating chambers of their own bodies. To Native Americans, this ability symbolizes the ability to use sound to balance and heal humans on the emotional and physical levels. And whales represent the potential for humans in awakening their own inner depths.

The image of a whale breaching evokes the most primordial secret of them all – how life began. A smooth, black behemoth rising from the mysterious and unknowable ocean depths to soar into the air, the whale represents the mystery of life itself as well as the mystery and glory of its inception. Thus whales are symbolic of creation to peoples all over the globe. The humpback whales' propensity to sing and its ability to change its song each year surely contributed to whales' symbolism of creativity. And because whales provide sustenance and survival in a harsh world, the Inuit regard whales as the greatest gift from the Great Spirit, proof that the Great Spirit loves them and provides for them in ways at once abundant and practical and yet mysterious and unpredictable.

Like countless people before me, my imagination was ignited by whales. It started as I watched the "Undersea World of Jacques Cousteau" Sunday nights on television as a young girl. By the time I was five years old, I'd already formed my dream of decoding whalesong. When I discovered Joan McIntyre's book "A Mind in the Waters" as a high school student, the mysteries of whales and the possibility of sharing consciousness with an animal so foreign and unlike me enticed me again. I lost myself in a world of newfound possibility and in the deep love the authors of the various pieces showed for the animals they studied and wrote about in the book.

My imagination was shelved for a while as I focused on becoming a scientist in college. For four and a half years, most of my brainpower was devoted to memorizing facts, writing papers, and reading text book after text book. But as I was about to graduate with my bachelor's degree, a new movie rekindled the flame: Star Trek IV – The Voyage Home. In this movie, the crew of the starship Enterprise returns to present-day San Francisco in order to locate a humpback whale who can communicate with a menacing alien probe floating through space in the future. In my favorite scene, Spock dives into the huge aquarium tank housing a humpback whale. He swims close to her and looks deeply into her large, brown eye and they have a conversation. After getting the information he wanted, he returns to the surface to confront a blustering Captain Kirk, who demands to know what he was doing. "Mind melding" was Spock's logical answer. Forever after, I dreamed of mind melding with a whale (or any other animal I could find, for that matter). Spock made it seem so simple, so logical, so elementary. My imagination enveloped me in a cloud of possibility. Just below the level of my awareness, my Dr. Doolittle dream was bubbling again.

Because I grew up (part of the time) in a beach town on the northern California coast, the whale that I am most familiar with is the Gray Whale. I've seen their vertebrae partially buried in the sand on a winter beach walk, heard countless reports of their migration patterns on TV and radio, and watched them myself through binoculars from the edge of coastal cliffs as they migrated from their Alaskan feeding grounds south to the warm lagoons of Mexico to deliver the babies they carried and make new ones.

Gray whales (scientific name, *Eschrichtius robustus*) are small and plain as whales go. At 52 feet and 36 tons, they are roughly half the size of the blue whale, the largest whale and the largest animal to ever live on Earth. (Yes, they really are larger than any dinosaur that ever lived, as I have to repeatedly explain to my 5 year old, dino-loving son.) Their common name is simply descriptive of the mottled gray color of their bodies. Their scientific name means "big Eschricht" and they were named in 1865 by taxonomist John Edward Gray after his friend, zoologist Daniel Eschricht. Whales have been hunted in large-scale whaling operations since the 17th century for their oil, meat and baleen (which was used to make corsets for women). To whalers of the 19th century, gray whales were known as "devil fish" due to the frantic way they fought off their hunters. Now that they are protected from hunting, gray whales can expect to live for 50 to 70 years.

Gray whales are one of the fifteen species of baleen whales, toothless whales that use huge baleen plates hanging from the tops of their mouths to filter small fish and krill out of the water to eat. Although baleen whales live in all the world's oceans, gray whales are now found only in two distinct populations, both in the Pacific Ocean. The North American population summers in Alaska and winters in Mexico and seems to be a relatively stable group with about 20,000 individuals. The other population is the critically endangered Asian population that ranges from the Sea of Okhotsk (a body of water located between Russia and Japan) and the coast of South Korea. Less is known about this population but it appears to consist of only 160 individuals. Gray whales used to live in two Atlantic Ocean populations: one along the European coast (until about 500AD) and the other along the American coast (until about 1800). Both of these populations were probably decimated by human hunters.

On November 24, 2010, I decide to try shape shifting into a gray whale form. From a chair at my dining room table, I float my awareness out of my body and across the state of California to the coast. It's the fall and I know the Gray Whales are migrating down the coast, I've seen them passing by several times from the beach or the cliffs overlooking the ocean. I focus my attention on the ocean near the Point Reyes Lighthouse, a place where I've watched them migrate close to shore. And then it happens, I connect with a Gray whale migrating from Alaska to Mexico, bringing my consciousness into her body and sharing her experience.

The first thing I am aware of is a strong sense of rhythm – feeling pulled to the south, the rhythm of the seasons, the rhythm of travel, the rhythm of breathing. I have an awareness of where other whales are located in space relative to me. I feel one farther offshore, one a mile or two behind me and one in front of me about the same distance away as the one behind me. I feel like I can feel their presences in the pressure of the water on my body. I also feel a sense of surrender to a force greater than myself, a "present-in-the-momentness." It feels very calm and very Zen.

My awareness is such a huge field around me. I think it is my body – so big – but it feels larger even than that and it seems to include my energetic awareness of my friends and family. There is a knowingness of what is to come and what I had just left, but no sense of excitement or anticipation, just being present in what was going on right now. Words bounce into my head. "Cycles. Rhythms. Seasons. Surrender to what is. Be here now." As I type these words at my computer now and re-connect to the experience, my thoughts are coming to me in rhythm and my body is swaying, pulsing to that rhythm.

My shoulders feel very far apart and really small. I can feel my hands/fins pointing backward. From my eyes to my shoulders, it feels smooth, like a single line, streamlined but with lots of tingling awareness and energy. I feel a peaceful sense of joy and of belonging, knowing my place in the world, the natural order of things. I feel very open and aware, with an expanded consciousness. I know that this whale would be fully present in any moment. Mexico is a time for fun and socializing, Alaska a time for feasting and being close. Travel is a more solitary time. All of these times are good and appreciated in their own way. I come to the surface to breathe, exhale powerfully, and then take a deep, slow breath and feel peace flood through my body, filling up my body and my consciousness.

I sense the waves breaking on the shore to my left. Even if I couldn't see, even if I were in pitch blackness, in the middle of the inkiest black of a starless night, I would know where I am. To my left, I feel the pull of the energy moving through the waves breaking on the shoreline; I feel the pull of the open ocean, wide and deep, to my right. When I pass the Golden Gate, I will feel the open pull of San Francisco Bay, a new rhythm of energy in the water to my left. My whole body is like an energy detector so I am aware of subtle energetic fields and changes in those fields.

I ask this gray whale my three questions and her answers move me powerfully. She views her spiritual gift as peace, equanimity and being truly alive in the present moment, with no attachment to past or future. I can really feel this as I share her awareness with her. The spiritual lesson follows the themes of cycles and surrender. The lesson and challenge of the gray whale is following the deeper inner pull of cycles, traditions, and forces stronger than the individual. Her message to humans is to love and cherish the oceans, which she reminds us are deep, powerful, and mysterious. "Respect the power and the unknown. Please keep it clean and healthy. We know the changes that are taking place globally with pollution and just ask that you bring awareness to your actions. Actions have consequences. We need to stay clean to be healthy and thrive and live our lives. We ask for your help."

Just as the largest living land animal the elephant did, the largest living marine animal is asking for our help. But she is not angry like the elephants. She is making a peaceful request. I am struck by the similarity of the messages from the elephants and the whale. The bull elephant said "we need to be ourselves to be healthy" and the whale is saying that whales need to be healthy to be themselves. Whales are swimming in a sea of our pollution – chemical, physical and acoustic. For eons the ocean has had the ability to clean itself and recycle any toxins that found their way into it. But now our pollution rate is exceeding the regeneration rate of the ocean and affecting the health of all the species that live there.

The Canadian government identified eight main threats to the North American population of gray whales. All of them are anthropogenic (created by humans). The first is the increase in human activity in their breeding lagoons in Mexico that could affect breeding success and the survival rates for young calves. Entanglement with fishing gear and boat collisions are two more concerns. Whaling by aboriginal groups in Canada and Alaska could also impact their numbers. Underwater noise pollution, the threat of toxic spills, impacts from fossil fuel exploration and extraction are major threats from humanity. Finally, climate change could affect the whales' food sources and other factors that could impact their survival. North American Gray whales are protected under Canada's Species at Risk Act, Mexican laws, and the U.S. Endangered Species Act. But this might not be enough for them. Legislation may keep their numbers stable but it may not ensure the quality of life that the whales want that comes with clean water to live in, clean air to breathe, and clean food to eat. We may need to do more.

What more can we do? Because of their size and their need to migrate, we can't just pluck a few whales out of the ocean and hold them in reserve until we get our oceans cleaned up. We've been able to do this successfully for several species of land mammals, but marine mammals present challenges to conservation that are going to be hard to overcome. Whales are at our mercy. We are faced with a mind in the waters that has achieved a level of peace and consciousness that we as a species have not achieved ourselves. Our planet is getting close to the tipping point, the point of no return where the scales tip the other way and the global changes move past the point of our ability to navigate and manage them. This gray whale is asking us to simply bring awareness to our actions. What are the decisions and actions I am making today that might impact the whales? Can I make a different decision or choose a different course of action that might lessen the negative impact on our watery friends? These are the questions to ask ourselves regularly.

As a child I dreamed of understanding what whales were saying in their songs. I haven't done that yet, but just maybe I'm on the right track and I will someday. My imagination in this direction was ignited again by a book that I recently re-read (for the fourth or fifth time, I've lost count). *Fluke* by Christopher Moore is a novel about Nate Quinn, a marine biologist studying humpback whale songs. Completely stumped after twenty years of steady research and inquiry, Nate has an extraordinary experience that gives him the insight that when the whales are singing they are praying to their Great Spirit. And their prayers are being answered. What are they praying for? Food. He demonstrates this by taking a sample of ocean water into an office and playing recorded humpback whales songs to it. Small shrimp called krill spontaneously generate in the water. Nate is so moved by his discovery that he closes his scientific investigation, buys a large boat, and devotes his life to saving whales around the world. These whales are praying and their prayers are being answered, he declares. How can we, he reasons, justify doing anything that could harm such evolved beings? We can't, he concludes, and his work for the rest of his life is set before him.

LITTLE BROWN BAT, *Myotis lucifugus*

Bats are small, nocturnal, social mammals living in colonies. They are the only mammals who can truly fly. (Flying squirrels use extra skin between their limbs and their trunks to glide to another tree or the ground from a higher perch, usually in a tree.) Most bats eat insects and or pollinate plants. They have excellent vision and all but one species (the diurnal fruit-eating bats called the giant flying foxes) also have the ability to use echolocation to detect their prey. The old wives tale of "blind as a bat" is just not true. Bats' eyes are well-developed. Their sonar ability doesn't exist because they can't see in the dark but to enhance their regular vision.

Like most biologists, I have a healthy interest in all animals, including bats. Whenever I see a wild animal of any kind, a kind of special awe comes over me. I'm fascinated by the myriad ways there are to be a living creature on this planet. Since moving to northern California seven years ago, bats have popped into my life from time to time. My husband and I like to take our family to Lake Tahoe in the winter and the summer. One of the treats of hiking or simply walking in the forests at night is the opportunity to watch bats flying overhead, hunting insects. If we're very quiet, we can sometimes hear the high pitched squeaks that they emit as they fly.

I consider myself extremely lucky to live at the edge of the rolling foothills and volcanic canyons that surround the great Central Valley of California. On warm summer nights, I will sometimes take a quick ride through our local open-space park for a cooling dip in the creek that runs through it. On my way home, I almost always see bats as I cross a bridge over the lower part of the creek. "What's it like to live in such a three-dimensional world?" I wonder to myself as I slow to watch the spectacle of the bats emerging for their nightly hunt. Deer often graze nearby, searching for the sweet shoots of grass surfacing in the fairways of the local golf course. As the bats disperse and roam beyond my view, I continue on my way with a contented smile, knowing that all is well in my world because I share it with many different kinds of animals.

On one of our fieldtrips last fall, Ellery and I were driving around town, trying to figure out an animal species to talk to. We listed the sheep and cattle farms on the south and north ends of town, the live animals housed at the Nature Center in the park, the Farm Sanctuary in the neighboring town. None seemed right. Finally, we hit on the bats I sometimes see on summer bike rides. We would go to their bridge and attempt to communicate intuitively with them so I could ask them my three questions.

The first thing I felt as I stood at the end of the bridge was a group blanket of energy, a sense of strategic hunting, and warmth, trust, connection, knowing and family. I sent a ribbon of my energetic awareness down toward the creek and then up under the bridge. As soon as my awareness reached the roost, I immediately felt the connection of being plugged into the community, along with the warmth of the other bats. The group felt friendly, warm, and welcoming, with an energetic awareness of my presence. I knew that each bat knew I was there the second I arrived. And just as quickly I felt them welcoming me. I rested upside down with the group, noticing how it felt to be so transparent. It was a very full, rich feeling that was somehow comforting and relaxing. There was no artifice here, no need to impress. I was known and accepted exactly as I honestly was.

Moments later, the group flew out from under the bridge to hunt as if it were dusk and I went with them. The group spread out but stayed connected with each other, immersed in the total knowledge of where each individual was and how many bugs of which species were around them. From my energetic awareness flying with them, I was looking down on the park from above, the creek off to my left, the golf course stretching up the sloping hills to my right. Superimposed over the natural features was a three-dimensional map of lines and angles and vectors that contained all the knowledge of the group in it. Parabolas in glowing green lines indicated the relative abundance of the insects near each bat. The images reminded me of the maps of air traffic controllers or sonar technicians on submarines or pilots using computer enhancement screens. There were many levels of information – where everyone was, what they were doing, what species of insects they were with, and how big the insect swarm was.

In this group, there was no sense of competition at all. They all kept track of each other so that each individual maximized his or her hunting gains. I got the sense that if one bat was in a small patch, it would know where more bugs were and would go there but no one would go somewhere that there wasn't enough food for them. There was real intimacy in this group.

When I asked them my questions, the bats told me that their first spiritual gift is the ability to surrender to the present moment. Nothing else exists except for what is happening now and how the bat relates to it. They said their second gift is the ability to be part of and to utilize a community mind. Each bat shares its knowledge through a collective consciousness within the colony.

Their spiritual lesson is accepting the reality that for them there is nowhere to hide, nowhere to be alone. Through selflessness, surrender to the group, connections between group members, and community efforts (such as raising babies together), there is a blurring of individuals within the group. It's hard to tell where one stops and another begins. Each individual is always visible and known to the group. I had felt this strongly the moment I entered the roost.

The message from Little Brown bats to humans is to "slow down and be present. Family and community come first and give the greatest joys and comforts. Feel the pulse of the collective group energy and intelligence. The whole is greater than the sum of the parts."

Most of the ancients couldn't have been more wrong when they chose the symbolism of bats. In ancient Babylonia, bats represented the souls of the dead. The ancient Mayans regarded bats as a symbol of initiation and rebirth and this view is still followed today in many modern Native American traditions. According to the Medicine Cards, a Native American divination system, bats represent rebirth, reflecting a shaman's death and initiation in secrecy or breaking down your former self through intense tests. The bats' ability to hang upside down to sleep corresponds to the ability to transpose the self into a newborn being (since hanging upside down is the same position that human babies are born in). Bats can also represent the rebirth of some part of yourself or the death of old patterns. In the book *Animal Speak,* author Ted Andrews notes that bats represent transition and initiation, the ability to face your fears and prepare for change.

According to the author, when bat shows up in your life "you are being challenged to let go of the old and create the new."

Maybe these philosophers were familiar with a different species of bats than the ones I encountered. It's possible that different species have different biology, different cultures, different experiences, and different spiritual gifts and lesson. But I couldn't help thinking that we humans really missed the boat on this one. In China, however, bats represented happiness and a long life. This one I can understand based on my experience with the bats that live near me. They seemed content, safe in the knowledge that they knew who they were and where they stood. They were known and loved and supported by their community members. Surely these attributes would contribute to happiness and a long life. Chalk one up to the ancient Chinese.

In my opinion, little brown bats are really all about intimacy. I am all about independence. My personal message from the bats (my interpretation of their message to my own life) is to stop isolating myself, to share myself openly with my friends, family and community. My tai chi teacher years ago lent me a book called "There Are No Secrets." The message of this book to me was that it's all out there; all of our personal information is available in our energy fields. The converse is true, too: everything we want to know is available to us, too. The only secret we keep is with ourselves through our illusion of privacy. We are known. Who we are is visible to others. Often strangers and friends recognize truths about us before we ourselves recognize them. For a lot of my life I've felt like an outsider, sometimes even a loner. The bats reminded me that I am in a community and I am known. And that's okay.

When I shared my project with my teachers and my classmates in February, I had already asked my three questions to animals in twenty different species. Ron asked me which animal was the biggest surprise. Without hesitation, I replied that it was the bat. The reality that I experienced was so radically different from how they are portrayed in modern movies and ancient mythology that I was completely blown away.

The intimacy, the knowing and acceptance of each bat for each other bat was amazing and heartwarming and humbling to share. The love and support was palpable and the remarkable discovery for me was that there was no competition. Anywhere. In my family, it sometimes feels like we were all competing with each other. As kids, my brothers and sister and I were competing for attention from our busy parents. As adults, we competed at family gatherings to be the funniest or the most popular or the thinnest or the most whatever. There was always a subtle undercurrent of competition in my family. Maybe it really existed. Maybe it was all in my mind, but it was there and real for me. To be in a family with no competition when I was among the bats was quite a revelation. "Wow. This is how our world could be, too," I thought to myself. And that special experience has shaded all of my interactions since. If the specter of competition enters my mind, I notice it, recognize it, and let it go. I thank the bats for that.

I understand the bats' challenge of being totally known all the time and how the transparency on that end of the spectrum would be hard to take, but for someone whose "lone wolf" persona had ruled her life and her interactions with her family for over forty years, the intimacy was appealing. Bats hold a special place in my heart now. How can they not? My experience with them was so dramatic and their message resonated with me so deeply.

In March, Chris and I took our kids to Disney World for the week of Spring Break. Towards the end of the week, we went to Animal Kingdom for the second time. On this day, we did the walking safari tour. My daughter Alexis was very drawn to the Komodo dragon in the first enclosure. Its colors were striking and it was so large that she marveled at its beauty and its power. At the next stop, we viewed a colony of two species of bats. One of the species was a small fruit bat and the other was the largest species of bats, the flying fox. Oh, my god! Their wings were so amazing. The thin, rubbery, leathery black tissue strung between hooking claws and extended fingers looked soft and flexible and elastic and shiny and foreign to me. It was so enticing I couldn't stop looking at the bats' wings. I wanted to touch them, to feel that soft leathery skin stretch against my hand. I pictured the outline of my hand on the other side as I pressed against an open expanse of bat wing. I marveled at the grappling hooks that curved out of their elbows. With a sharp black nail at the end, it looked like it could do serious damage to delicate flesh. My face pressed against the screen separating the viewing area from the roosting area, I took picture after picture with our small family camera, trying to get a closer look at the details of their bodies.

One bat was hanging upside down twenty feet overhead – hanging by one nail of one single digit, its other fingers curled gently next to it in mid-air. It seemed to be asleep! Its eyes were closed and it appeared oblivious of its impending impact with the concrete flooring below, a potential impact that twisted my stomach up in knots. Eventually, I couldn't stand the tension and had to look away. Before I left dozens of minutes later, I glanced back and, of course, the bat was fixed in the same place in the same position.

Another bat was walking foot over foot along a tightrope strung across the enclosure. Upside down, it seemed entirely comfortable detaching and reattaching the claws of each foot as it made its way who knows where and who knows why. My husband nudged me, letting me know that he and the kids were moving on. "Uh, okay," I mumbled back to him as I snapped another photo. When I joined them several minutes later, after talking to the naturalist on duty and asking every question I could think of (interspersed with ooh's and aaah's about how magnificent these animals are), my husband commented wryly, "I thought you were going to stay there all day." I could have, I thought to myself, if it weren't for the kids. We're here for the kids, I'd reminded myself and forced myself to re-join my own all-knowing family unit. That evening, Chris was looking through the photos of the day on our digital camera. "Are there any of Lexi and Zane?" I asked. "One or two," was his good-natured reply. When we got home, I looked through all our pictures. I'd taken more pictures those bats that one morning than I had of my family all week!

I think Ted Andrews was right when he wrote that when bat shows up in your life "you are being challenged to let go of the old and create the new." Since I really met my bat neighbors, I have let go of my old beliefs about them and my old ways of being myself. I am in the process of creating new understanding and new ways of interacting in my life. The bats have truly opened my eyes to see in a new, richer, more loving way.

GREAT GRAY OWL, *Strix nebulosi*

It's a sunny Wednesday afternoon outside as Ellery and I sit at her breakfast table drinking tea and paging through the books I've brought with me for our weekly field trip. As I left my house for our meeting, I grabbed my "Birds of Northern California" and "Field Guide to California Animals" books. For reasons I can't explain, today I am drawn to birds in general and owls in particular.

Owls are medium sized birds that live throughout the world in a variety of habitats. They are divided into two categories: typical owls (scientific family Strigidae) and barn owls (scientific family Tytonidae). Owls tend to be solitary and nocturnal. They are carnivores who hunt insects, rodents and rabbits, although some owls specialize on hunting fish. Although owls have binocular vision, their large eyes are fixed in their sockets. Owls, like all birds, must turn their entire head to change views. Owls, however, have an advantage over other bird species: they can rotate their heads and necks as much as 270 degrees in either direction.

As a nocturnal bird, owls have always represented mystery as well as the darkness within. Through their association with the moon, they are also considered to be symbols of the feminine (and fertility), the moon, and the night. According to Ted Andrews in

Animal Speak, "the owl is the bird of magic and darkness, of prophecy and wisdom."

In modern and ancient Africa, owls are considered harbingers of ill health, bad luck and death. In Arab cultures they are considered bad omens. Many Native American traditions associate owls with evil, death, destruction and dark supernatural forces. The Pawnee, however, saw the owl as a symbol of protection. The Pueblo associated owls with the Skeleton Man, their god of death as well as the spirit of fertility.

In the modern West (including ancient Greece and contemporary America), owls are associated with wisdom. In Ancient Greece, the owl was a symbol for the city-state of Athens as well as its patron goddess Athena, who was also the goddess of wisdom. In Ancient Rome, an owl's feather placed on a sleeping person had the power to enable a person to learn the secrets of the sleeping person.

In the kitchen with Ellery, I learn from my books that thirty-seven species of owls live in the US, Canada and Mexico. One owl species in particular seems especially attractive and appealing, the great gray owl, and I can't tear my eyes away from its picture in the guide book. The Great Gray Owl (scientific name *Strix nebulosa*) is the largest of all the North American owls. I learn that the great gray owl is the provincial bird of Manitoba, Canada and that the species name "*nebulosa*" comes from a Latin word meaning misty or foggy. This could be a reference to the fuzzy outline they make when they fly silently through the evening or night sky. This is the bird that I want to contact today.

Unlike their more famous cousins the spotted owl (*Strix occidentalis*) that live in coastal old growth forests, the Great Gray

Owl lives in boreal forests with coniferous trees (pine and other trees with needle-like leaves), snowy winters, and short summers. In some areas Great Gray owls are also called the Great Gray Ghost or the Phantom of the north. Great Gray owls hunt mostly in early morning and late afternoon, and they are one of the few species of owls that could be seen hunting at any time of the day or night.

Great Gray owls are long-lived birds, with captive owls living up to 40 years. Deaths of wild birds are most often due to starvation. The natural enemies of Great gray owls (Great Horned Owls, martens (a type of weasel), and wolverines) prey on juveniles. Human interactions take their toll on these owls, too, through shootings, road kills, and electrocutions.

Ellery and I decide to independently connect with the owl and share our experiences with each other afterward. From my chair at Ellery's kitchen table, I close my eyes and float my awareness up above her house and across northern California to a forest south of Lake Tahoe. I quickly feel my awareness settle into the form of a male owl perched in a tree.

As I shift from my normal awareness of myself to my owl awareness, I recognize that the sixth chakra of the owl is very strong, which suggests heightened mental abilities and possibly even clairvoyance. I gradually begin to notice how I feel and what I know. First, I notice that I have clear vision, sharp hearing, acute senses and keen awareness. I feel the gentle strength of my owl body. I have no hesitation – my decisions are made instantly, with great awareness and clarity. In my owl mind, I have an encyclopedic knowledge of my prey animals and their life cycles, habits, and even family connections. I know what death is and how prey feels fear and loss at death. I know the consequences of my hunting on the one I capture and those left behind. But my own needs come first, even with this knowing.

I alight from the tree and suddenly I am flying through a clearing between trees, a meadow made by the fairway of a golf course. It's lined with forest on both sides. I stretch out my wings and float through the cool, thin air. The feathers on my belly ruffle in the breeze, but the rest of me remains motionless, unaffected by the movement or the breeze created as my body passes through the still air. Silently, I bank and turn, searching the earth below me, watching the trees rise and fall by my sides as I change my altitude. I'm surprised that I don't even hear the wind whistling through my wing feathers, but then I remember that the leading edge of great gray owl's flight feathers is serrated to minimize noise when flying, helping them to be stealthy hunter.

The ground is blanketed by a thick foot of snow. I know where my prey is under the snow. From the high pitched sounds I hear, I visualize a maze of gray shadowy tunnels under the snow. My intended prey is traveling through these tunnels quietly, but not quietly enough to escape detection by my sensitive ears. I hear their movements, knowing as I do where to look and listen and focus my attention. I effortlessly integrate my knowledge and experience with the information coming into my senses in this moment.

Once prey is captured, it is killed by a combination of tearing soft tissue with the beak and crushing the skull with the talons. The beak of the owl is short, hooked at the tip, and curved downward. The downward-facing beak allows a clear field of vision, and helps direct sound waves toward the ears. Owls often swallow their prey whole and regurgitate the indigestible parts (such as bones, scales and fur) in the form of pellets. These "owl pellets" are plentiful and are often sold to schools for dissection by students. Students can easily identify prey ingested by the owl as a dynamic way to understand ecology and relationships between different species of animals.

After the hunt is complete, I ask the owl my three questions. He tells me that the spiritual gifts of the Great Gray Owl are swiftness, sureness, and clarity of vision, knowledge, and action. Their spiritual lesson is an unbearable compassion from having the burden of the ages. As sentries and witnesses they see all with knowledge, understanding, and "unbearable compassion." These owls integrate intellect and emotion and experience both fully, with the added ability to put themselves in other animal's "shoes." They are able to understand and empathize with the suffering of other animals, even those that they must kill in order to survive.

The great gray owl's message to humans is to know where you fit in the world, see clearly. Don't delude yourself: actions have consequences – you may have to lose one thing to gain something else. They prey loses its life as the predator gains food, energy, warmth, knowledge, and experience. There is more than one side to a coin. Sometimes you must pay a toll, pay a price for what you want. But you must do it anyway. You must not cheat yourself out of your due. Don't delude yourself. Take care of yourself and accept the consequences.

The great gray owl is a perfect model of wisdom. According to Erickson, wisdom is knowledge passed through the crucible of experience. The great gray owl has integrated information and experience as well as awareness and compassion. The human age stage associated with wisdom is the retirement years of sixty-five and beyond. A fully integrated adult human at this stage has compassion and caring as well as actualized information, wisdom.

For me, the message of the great gray owl is to drop over-responsibility, take care of yourself and make your own choices. "To thine own self be true," as Shakespeare said. We humans have been getting this message for centuries and yet it is still a hard one to internalize and make real in our lives. When I am confronted with difficult decisions, I think of the owl and the clarity of his vision and understanding. Somehow, the owl's message makes it easier for me to make difficult decisions that impact other people in uncomfortable ways. It helps me find a place of compassion and clarity inside of me so I can find the decision that is right for me.

I am reminded of Steven Covey's "sphere of influence." There is part of our world that we can actually impact or influence; this is where our actions are most effective. Everywhere else in the world is outside our influence. If we concentrate on acting within our sphere of influence, we become more effective people. If we try to act outside our sphere of influence, we cause ourselves stress and suffering. The owl recognizes what it can and can't influence. The owl is living the prayer, "God, grant me the strength to change the things I can, to accept those I can't and the wisdom to know the difference." The owl knows what can be influenced and what can't.

Unfortunately, we humans have tremendous impact on great gray owls. Their greatest conservation threat is timber harvesting in their habitats. Deforestation typically reduces the number of live and dead large-diameter trees these birds use for nesting. It also takes away the leaning trees juvenile owls use for roosting before they are able to fly. Finally, timber harvesting decreases the dense canopy used by juveniles for cover and protection from predators. Although conservationists have introduced human-made versions of these missing trees after harvesting, and some owls have used them, great gray owls are far more common in areas protected from logging. Livestock grazing in meadows also adversely affects Great Grey Owls, by reducing habitat for their preferred prey species.

The great gray owl has been one of my favorite animals to meet during this past year. Its wisdom and compassion really touched my heart and resonated with me. This owl lives the way I would like to live. Once I connect with an animal in this way, I want to do all I can to help it. That is why I am ending this chapter with conservation information about the great gray owl. I want everyone to know how they can help this wise owl. There is an intersection of biology, humanity and spirituality that is very real. Owls are important piece of the natural ecology of their habitat. They are also powerful spiritual symbols for humans. Both aspects of their lives are important for us to be aware of. Without owls, we lose a part of ourselves and the mystery of life and we lose important ecological component of our ecosystem.

CATS, Felis catus

I have a confession to make: I am not a cat person. Let me be really honest about that right up front. I've already confessed to being a dog person, so it probably comes as no surprise that I don't consider myself a cat person, but I just wanted to be honest about it at the outset of this chapter. I'm allergic to all animals with fur (making it easy to become a marine biologist) and although I've overcome my allergy to dogs for the most part by using homeopathic remedies, I've never attempted to address my allergy to cats. I am fine with living with dogs and without cats. No animosity, but I don't really feel like I'm missing out, either. Except for maybe the kittens. They are so cute and it would be really nice to be able to hold and pet those adorable little balls of fluff. Many of my friends have cats and many of my clients ask me to do readings for their cats, so I have learned to appreciate the personalities and idiosyncrasies of cats.

Domesticated cats have been living with humans for thousands of years. They are clearly depicted in Egyptian paintings roughly 3,600 years old. Historians used to believe that cats were first domesticated in ancient Egypt, but recent genetic studies suggest that all house cats are descended from African wildcats (*Felis silvestris lybica*). Some taxonomists classify domesticated cats as a subspecies of wildcats, using the scientific name *Felis silvestris catus*.

In 2004, a Neolithic grave estimated to be 9,500 years old was excavated in Cyprus. The grave contained the skeletons of a human and a cat. This is the oldest recorded close association between humans and cats. The cat skeleton closely resembles an African wildcat.

The dominant theory of the domestication of wildcats into house cats is that they were "self-domesticating," initiating their own association with humans during the Agricultural Revolution. When farmers in the "Fertile Crescent" of the Near East started storing grains in granaries that attracted rodents, cats were drawn in to the easy source of concentrated food. Humans tolerated the cats and gradually a mutual relationship evolved.

During the Age of Discovery, cats were brought on sailing ships to control shipboard rodents and to serve as good-luck charms. Today, cats are one of the most popular pets in the world. There are an estimated 500 million house cats in the world and they are found in nearly every country around the globe.

Cats have excellent hearing, smell and night vision. Despite being solitary hunters, cats are also a social species. They use vocalizations, pheromones (chemicals produced in their bodies), and body language to communicate. Their vocalizations include meowing, purring, trilling, hissing, growling, and grunting.

Cats had special rank and privilege and were even worshipped in ancient Egypt as sacred animals. The Egyptian goddess Bast was often depicted in the form of a cat. In Scandinavia, cats are associated with the goddess of fertility, Freyja, and the Hindu goddess of childbirth, Shasthi, is shown riding on a cat. In Japan, the Maneki Neko is a cat that is a symbol of good fortune. Although cats represent magic, mystery and independence in Native American symbolism, one practical and insightful Native American proverb warns that "After dark all cats are leopards."

The natural suppleness and swiftness of cats helps them to escape seemingly life-threatening situations. No matter how great the height, falling cats are able to right themselves mid-air and land on their feet, an ability that likely led to the myths in many cultures that cats have multiple lives. In the US and many other countries, they are said to have nine lives, but in some Spanish-speaking regions they are said to have seven lives. In Turkish and Arabic traditions, cats are said to have six lives.

In the United States, we have lots of popular sayings about cats. "Curiosity killed the cat" is meant as a warning to people to be careful about what they'll uncover. A black cat crossing your path is considered bad luck. And every child knows that a cat is the familiar animal of a witch.

On Friday, February 25, 2011, it snowed in the central valley of California at a few minutes after eight o'clock in the morning. I had just dropped my two kids off at school and was walking back to my car when a cheer broke out in the school yard: the light rain had turned to fluffy, white snow. Large flakes were floating down and melting on the asphalt as school children turned their heads toward the sky and opened their mouths, hoping to catch snowflakes on their tongues. I smiled at the wonderment of life and how such a simple thing can bring such excitement and joy to children.

When I got in my car, I started to plan my day. I immediately realized that I had only one animal left to interview for this book: a cat. I flashed on my friend Michele who has been a loving supporter of me and this book for a long time. She has shared in my journey, buoying me up when I was pessimistic and celebrating with me when I was excited. She was a great friend and she had a cat. How perfect, I thought to myself, if I could ask my three questions to her cat. I immediately called her on my cell phone and woke her up. Oops! But she said, sure, come on over! That sounds great!

We huddled near her woodstove drinking tea and eating cereal for breakfast as the storm continued outside. I felt like I was floating in a warm cocoon in the middle of a light, fluffy snow storm. The wind would scrape tree branches against the house occasionally, but it was a soft and gentle snow that felt like a cozy gray and white blanket around us. Bianca the cat wandered around the house, not paying any attention to us as we caught up with each other and enjoyed our morning.

When our social hour was complete and I asked Bianca what the spiritual gift of cats is, she replied poetically, "sleek and swift like moonlight on the grass; focused attention; the huntress on the prowl." This reminded me of the Indian proverb that "A cat is a lion in a jungle of small bushes."

She told me that her spiritual lesson is balancing autonomy with connection to people. Bianca says her challenge is "walking between two worlds – mine and the humans' – and it's hard to communicate my needs and desires." When I asked her if it was the same for all cats, she said, "Yes, we all have the challenge of the balance between independence/autonomy and connecting with our people. Where is the line? It can shift and sway and move away." Bianca was the most poetic animal I had encountered!

I asked Bianca if she had a message to share with people. Here, she was much more straightforward: "Give us what we want and then leave us alone to do our thing." I almost laughed out loud! When I shared all of Bianca's responses with Michele and her husband Rex, we all had a good laugh together. Right there, Bianca had captured the essence of cats. I think any cat lover can relate to Bianca's sentiment and has probably seen it played out over and over in their lives.

Bianca's answers to my questions made sense to me in light of the theoretical "self-domesticating" history of cats. They still see themselves as fearless, independent hunters. Her message to humans could have been voiced by the first cats to feed at the first granaries. Cats still struggle with the challenge of balancing their instinctive solitary hunting nature with thousands of years of domestication. What an interesting spiritual challenge to take on!

Part of my journey this year has been to build closer relationships with a variety of animals that I had had little contact with in the past, such as snakes, bats and lions. Cats are one of those animals, too. This year, I've had the opportunity to help reunite three families with their lost cats. The first was for a friend in San Diego, the third was for a classmate in Los Angeles, and the second was an "accident" that almost didn't happen. Here is how that experience went:

I drove across town toward my friend Analia's house. We had a date to go see Maya Angelou speak and we were both excited. About a mile away from my house, I realized that I had forgotten my purse with the tickets in it. I turned around, thinking "This isn't like me..." When I arrived at Analia's, I apologized for being late, telling her that I had forgotten my purse with the tickets.

We chatted, ate some dinner and left her house with 40 minutes to complete the ten minute walk to the theater. We were relaxed and having a good time. Two blocks from her house, Analia asked me, "Do you have the tickets?" I started laughing out loud. I'd forgotten my purse again! As we turned around, I thought, "This *really* isn't like me…" At her driveway, we were distracted and stopped to watch a group of really cool ants for a few minutes. I was reminded that I had started a new book that morning called "Animal Omens" all about what it means metaphysically when different kinds of animals show up in your life. I remembered the ants' message was to share your gifts with the community.

We started off again, purse and tickets firmly in hand. At the end of the block, we saw two women posting "lost cat" fliers on the telephone pole. I looked at Analia and said, "This is why we kept getting waylaid." We started talking to the mother and her college-aged daughter about their cat. I told them that I was psychic. Before the words were even out of my mouth, the mother, Nancy, shoved the flier at me.

I looked at the picture of the black cat, closed my eyes, and asked the cat's name. When the daughter told me "Blanca," I giggled and I had to open my eyes, eyebrows raised, and say "Ironic!" to Analia. Eyes closed again, I connected with Blanca, and I could tell that she was okay and not too stressed. I saw her view of an orange house with an orange picket fence. It was on a northwest corner of a street.

As I shared the information, I looked around for the house, but couldn't see it. I re-connected with Blanca, asked for map, and got an aerial view of the neighborhood. I saw that Blanca was one block south and one block east of us. Curiously, I got a warm feeling emanating from that direction. I had never had that kind of warm feeling before. I shared the info again and Nancy and her daughter set off in the direction I had indicated.

Once again, Analia and I began our walk to Chico State. We made it to the theater just on time. Maya Angelou was fabulous, funny, and inspiring, a true national treasure.

The next day I received an email from Nancy saying, "Cara, I am the mother of the young woman with the lost cat last evening. You were right, we found her. Just where you directed. We knocked on doors and called to her. I felt a warm area and encouraged my daughter to call her friend. Kitty Blanca didn't come out right away. After I left for home, Acacia went back out on her bike calling her. Blanca came running. Pure magic is the only way I can describe running into you and your friend. Pure gratitude is what I feel for you helping my daughter on the spot. Thank you."

Cats have been another opportunity for me to relate to the world from a soul-centered perspective. I've been very touched by the love my friends and clients have for their cats. I love my dog in the same way, so I get it. I have a greater appreciation for cats now than I did a year ago. Cats are probably the animal that I lived most closely to but never really connected with before this project.

AFRICAN LION, *Panthera leo*

As a biologist and a woman, I've always been intrigued by sexual dimorphism in different species of animals. Sexual dimorphism (literally meaning "two body types based on gender") is the scientific term used to identify species in which males and females have physical differences in their body shape and/or size. Humans, for example, are sexually dimorphic. Dogs aren't. You can readily tell a male human from a female (well, most of the time!) but it takes a lot closer look to determine if a dog is male or female. Male and female elephant seals are dramatically different in size and appearance. (Males average 16 feet in length and weigh 6,000 pounds; females average 10 feet and 2,000 pounds.) African lions also have noticeable sexual dimorphism. The tallest of the four "big cats" in the genus *Panthera* (the other three are the tiger, the jaguar, and the leopard), African lions inhabit the open, grassy savannahs of Africa. Males are larger and have a distinctive mane after they reach maturity. Females are smaller than males and have no mane.

(Males aren't always larger than females in sexually dimorphic species. For most mammalian species, males are larger than females because they tend to fight for breeding rights or to defend their territories. In other species, females are larger than males. This is more common in species in which the female is responsible for birthing large numbers of offspring and she requires energetic resources that must be stored in her body. Many species of fish, insects and spiders show this pattern.)

In species with sexual dimorphism, the lifestyles of males and females (called "life history traits" in biology) are usually very different. Male lions, for instance, spend most of their lives alone or roaming with another male while females spend their entire lives with their pride, living with mothers, sisters, aunts and female cousins. Females also spend a lot of time and energy cooperatively hunting and raising their cubs. Males spend a lot of time and energy getting big. They need their size to defend their pride areas and to win and retain their positions as the leaders of their pride. When they can, adult males, alone or with a partner, will fight to take over a pride, driving out the existing male leader. They will then live in that pride until another males supplants them.

Another aspect of animal life that is noticeably different between the two sexes of a sexually dimorphic species is what biologists call "lifetime reproductive fitness." This fancy term just measures how many of an animal's offspring survive to have their own offspring. Male lions maximize their lifetime reproductive success by fathering as many cubs as they can. They do this by fighting to take over a pride and then killing all of the former leader's cub and mating with all the females to make new babies. (Females are only fertile after their babies have matured, which can take up to three years, so killing the babies brings the females into estrous sooner than would happen naturally.) Females maximize their lifetime reproductive success by taking very good care of the few babies that they will give birth to. After her babies are born, a mother will take care of them alone, away from the pride, for several weeks. After they are introduced to the pride, the babies will be raised cooperatively by all the adult females in the group.

The sexual dimorphism of males and females has led to two distinct body types, lifestyles, reproductive strategies, and survival pressures for lions. It has created distinct social and ecological roles as well. These gender differences have carried over to the way humans see animals and the way lions are recognized in spiritual symbolism. Male lions are known as "The King of the Beasts" and represent power, royalty and paternal leadership and wisdom. The lion symbolically presided over the annual floods of the Nile River in Egypt. In China, the male lion symbolizes protection and guardianship. The gold color of the lion represents the sun. The young lion symbolizes the rising sun (or rising son).

Lionesses represent the power of the feminine. The lioness also represents the sun, which gives birth to the new day and the energy of the sun that nurtures and warms life. According to Ted Andrews in Animal Speak, the lioness calls people to trust their feminine energy, the energy of creativity, intuition and imagination.

If the lives of male and female lions look so different to me and to the humans who created the meanings of their symbolism through the ages, I wonder how different they must feel to the lions themselves. When I began this project, I wondered if males and females of a species with pronounced sexual dimorphism would also have differences in the way they viewed their spiritual gifts and lessons. Because their daily lives are very different, they would be faced with different needs, challenges, decisions, and opportunities. Would these gender differences carry over into their spiritual make up, too? You can judge for yourself, because I asked my three questions to both an adult female lioness and an adult male lion.

On a cold, sunny, windy January day, Ellery and I drove two hours south of our town to talk to animals at the Sacramento Zoo. In the middle of the zoo, a lion and a lioness shared an enclosure and I intuitively asked them my three questions as I shivered and stomped my feet to keep warm. (We did take a mid-afternoon hot chocolate break to warm up and rest our brains.)

According to the lioness, her spiritual gift is doing it all. She has the full range of life experiences from mothering to hunting to killing. She loves her cubs and cares for and protects them but she also must hunt to provide her, her cubs, and her pride mates with food, killing whatever prey she is able to.

The spiritual lesson of the lioness is learning to surrender to what is with strength and endurance. As she put it to me, "Life isn't fair, so you do what you can do and you put up with it." Her message to people is to "be strong and don't think about the outcome, just do what you're called to do. Just take care of your part."

The spiritual gift of the male lion was very different from that of the lioness. According to the male lion at the Sacramento Zoo, his spiritual gift is strong, powerful, decisive leadership. He gets to be the boss, to be in charge and in command. His spiritual lesson is that good times are sure to end. He is not attached to anyone. He only has short stints at leading a pride with lots of lost-ness and aloneness in between. He likes to bask in the glory of the good times, but they are sure to end. His spiritual message to humans is "Dare to become as big as you dream of being. You can be great."

As I was writing this chapter, the subject of the differences between men and women came up repeatedly in casual conversations with my women friends. Out of the blue, when we'd been talking about school and work, one friend said to me that men can't be everything for women and women have to cultivate their relationships with other women in order to fulfill all their social and personal needs. Just like a lioness maintains relationships with the significant females in her life, human women often have their circle of close friends that they lean on for support, whether the support is emotional, physical, or practical such as sharing babysitting duties or helping to take care of a sick kid. Another friend, in a different conversation, observed how differently women and men approach our lives. It occurred to me that humans, with our sexual dimorphism, are not so different from lions with their sexual dimorphism. Men and women have different social roles and different life pressures and stresses. My husband's stress comes mainly from work and the pressures of paying the mortgage and other bills. My stress comes from taking care of my family.

I remember when my kids were born, everything changed for me. I went from an independent woman to a mom in the blink of an eye. I looked at absolutely everything in my life from a new perspective. My priority shifted from "what's in it for me?" to making my kids my priority and asking myself "how will this affect my family?" And some days, when one kid is sick and the other has a soccer game and I have to go to work and juggle a trip to the grocery store with laundry and walking the dog, I understand what the lioness means. You just do what you have to do. You take care of what's in front you. You don't have time or energy to "dare to become as big as you dream of being," as the male lions says. Some days there's just a lot of work to be done so you just do it.

When I was a kid, I was all about women's lib and equality. I wouldn't accept that there were biological differences between boys and girls and men and women. I rejected stereotypes that restricted women to homemakers and supporters of men in the workplace. I knew women had equivalent brains and strengths and gifts to offer the world. Studying biology has given me a greater appreciation the many different ways that different animals live. Through my training as a biologist, I released some of my judgments and pre-conceived notions about the world and about our social system. I still believe that every person should have equal opportunities to express themselves in their own unique ways. I think men should be able to stay home and raise the kids if that's what they want to do. Women should be able to run companies or countries if that's what they want to do. Women should also be able to stay home and raise kids if that's what they want to do without feeling judged or inferior in some way. Since I've had my own inner paradigm shift since having kids, I now embrace all the choices possible to everyone.

Exploring and experiencing the differences between male and female African lions has brought this issue to my awareness because to me the differences between lion and lioness illustrate one option for life on earth. There are many biological and spiritual opportunities available to souls. They choose the one that best fits their desired lessons and spiritual evolution. The African lion gives two distinct opportunities based on gender. Humans similarly offer different opportunities for personal and spiritual growth and life paths. The lions are helping me to see that one way is not better than another, they are just different.

SNAKE, Red Tailed Boa, Boa constrictor constrictor

Snakes come in all sizes from very small (Caribbean thread snakes are about 10 cm long) to almost unimaginably large (the reticulated python is the longest at 30 feet and the Anaconda is the heaviest at over 200 lbs.), but they all have the same, easily recognizable shape: long, thin, and cylindrical.

As I began writing this chapter, I thought to myself that I didn't really have much experience with snakes. As a graduate student, I'd had friends who were herpetologists and I never quite understood how their favorite animals could be snakes and lizards when there were such amazingly cool animals as dolphins on the planet. But I left them to their work. Then last week I started doodling a loose outline for this chapter. I didn't know that was what I was doing at the time; it's just what came out as I half listened to a class discussion. I'd always had a bit of a fear of snakes, not a phobia or anything, but certainly a sense of great caution when I was around them. Water snakes really creeped me out and I was definitely afraid of water moccasins and copper heads.

But I also had a fundamentally biological approach to all animals and my fascination with the myriad ways animals could be made overcame most of my trepidation. Mountain biking in North Carolina, a copper head crossed my path on a fast downhill. I braked hard but couldn't avoid him. I stopped my bike a few feet downhill, worried that I had hurt him. One of my companions said, "Only you would be worried that you had hurt a deadly snake!" Kayaking in South Carolina through a flooded forest, I passed within a few feet of a water moccasin coiled on a sawed off tree trunk. I gave it a lot of respect, but couldn't help but admire its shiny black scales and its serene presence – not a muscle moved as my companion and I paddled quietly past.

And then, of course, I recalled a chapter from my personal mythology: the story of how I met my husband. I had just finished writing the first draft of my master's thesis, having spent up to twelve hours per day writing on my small Macintosh computer for several weeks. I was ready for a break and went to the Yuba River for some solo camping and recuperation in nature. I spent a beautiful night next to the roaring water of Maytag Falls and then packed up and started making my way back home. I decided to stop and a read a book (a paperback no less!) at the confluence of the north and middle forks of the American River.

I placed my lawn chair on a gravel bar facing north, got out my book, and promptly fell asleep. As I slept, I had a dream that two snakes were moving towards me. They were a rosy sandy color that reminded me of a sun setting on a hazy night and they were identical, about two inches in diameter and four feet long. As they reached me, they separated and one snake coiled up and around each of my legs. When their faces got to my knees, I awoke from my dream. I opened my eyes and moving right under my chair, silently sliding past me between my feet, was a sandy tan snake. It was about the same dimensions as the snakes in my dream and just as stealthy. I watched it as it moved steadily away from me and then, about ten feet away, it turned toward the river and climbed a scraggly bush next to the water. "Huh," I thought to myself sleepily.

I remained still, but movement off to my left caused me to shift my gaze toward the hillside. Another identical snake was exiting the bushes on the hill, moving past the large boulders bordering the gravel bar toward me. The second snake roughly followed the path of the first and headed toward the river. A few minutes later, a third snake, smaller than the first two, made its way down the bank and to the water. I felt like just another piece of the landscape to these snakes. They paid no attention to me.

Wide awake now, interest in my book gone, I decided to go visit some friends in a nearby town. I was working during the summers as a whitewater rafting guide and my company had an outpost on the south fork of the American River. As I reached the warehouse, two men were just pulling away in a pickup truck. I recognized the passenger, flagged them down, hopped out of my truck and approached them. From outside the driver's window, I relayed my story to them, trying to catch the eye of the cute guy driving the truck, a stranger to me. The driver was shy, though, and wouldn't return my gaze, so I had to introduce myself after I finished sharing my story. This was the first meeting between me and my future husband, Chris.

With the exception of a few other chance encounters on rafting trips and research expeditions, that was the extent of my interactions with snakes before opening to my intuitive abilities. So it was surprising to me that seventeen years later one of the first animals I would communicate with intuitively would be a snake. This is how it happened. On September first, I began training with a running group for a 5K run. On September 29th, two weeks after my first conversation with Bear, I met a snake while I was running in a park. During a sunset training session, we were running on a path around a local grassy area created by two baseball diamonds and two soccer fields. At one end, some trees and bushes bordered the path. As I ran through this area, a coach was shooing runners to the outside of the path as a small garter snake crossed the path. I stopped to look at the snake as it traveled straight across the path about 5 feet in front of me. "Hi, snake!" I thought to it. The snake immediately made a ninety degree turn and headed straight toward me. "Uh oh!" I thought to myself. "What's this snake going to do?" Just then a group of runners jogged past me and the snake looked around nervously – he seemed to be trying to figure out what was going on. I knew the snake could feel the vibrations of the runners' feet pounding the pavement, but it was also moving its head from side to side, trying to see what was causing the ruckus. I sent the snake a picture of him going into the grass where he would be safe and he immediately turned ninety degrees again and slithered into the grass.

I continued on my run and when I returned to the spot where I had left him, I looked for the snake again. He was behind a tree with his head lifted off the ground, peering out at the runners. He seemed enthralled at the sight! On my next lap, the snake was gone, but as I ran on I heard a frog croaking in a flower bed and it occurred to me that there was a whole other reality in those flowers. What did the frog think of the unusual commotion? My consciousness was opened up by the snake's remarkable behavior and I had to consider the possibilities of what the animals living here thought about us.

Communicating intuitively with a snake was an early turning point for me in my journey this year. Snakes were animals that I didn't really relate to or think about much. I admired them from a biological point of view, from an evolutionary point of view, and sometimes from an aesthetic point of view, but I had never considered them from a spiritual point of view.

Of course other humans (and not just herpetologists) had been considering snakes and their spiritual or symbolic meaning for a long time. For most of us Westerners, the most famous snake is the one that lived in the Garden of Eden. Clearly, this snake represented the evils of temptation and dangers of giving in to our animal desires. But snakes have a more positive image in other cultures and spiritual traditions. They are a symbol of rebirth, resurrection, initiation, and wisdom in many Native American traditions. In ancient Mesoamerica, Quetzalcoatl, the feathered serpent deity, was the greatest of all the gods. Today, snakes adorn the symbol of medical doctors in America, representing wisdom through healing.

In some ancient Mediterranean religions, the snake was a symbol of the divine, representing wisdom and prophecy. Snakes were often kept in palaces and temples to bring luck or magic. In Greece, snakes represent alchemy and healing. Statues of a "snake goddess" – an elegantly dressed woman holding a snake in each hand – were found in Crete.

In India and Eastern religions, snakes represent sexuality and the creative life force– the kundalini energy rises up like a snake through the body. According to the "Yoga Kundalini Upanishad," written in the second century, "The divine power, Kundalini, shines like the stem of a young lotus; like a snake, coiled round upon herself she holds her tail in her mouth and lies resting half asleep as the base of the body." An entire branch of yoga practice practiced today is devoted to physically and energetically preparing and assisting the body to move kundalini energy up the back from the base of the spine to the crown of the head.

In ancient Egypt, Wadjet was the patroness of Lower Egypt who oversaw the lands and protected kings and women in childbirth. This goddess was represented as having the body of a woman with a snake's head (or the opposite, a snake with a woman's head) or simply as a snake. In the emblem of a snake joined with the sun disk, worn by all rulers of Lower Egypt, the snake represents Wadjet.

In Chinese astrology, snakes represent compassion, clairvoyance and charm. The Chinese "coiled dragon" symbol of a dragon eating its own tail common from roughly 5,000 to 3,000 BC was likely the precursor to the ouroborus, an ancient symbol of a snake devouring its own tail. Like the mythical phoenix rising out the ashes to be reborn again, the ouroborus also represents renewal and the cyclical nature of life.

I encountered my second snake to talk with at the Sacramento Zoo in January. The Red Tailed Boa (scientific name *Boa constrictor constrictor*) is one of ten subspecies of Boa Constrictors (scientific name *Boa constrictor*). They are found in woodlands, semi-arid forests and rain forests in Central and South America. Solitary animals, the boas live alone and only come together to mate. They give birth to 15 – 40 babies at a time. Unlike most snake species, boa babies are born alive; the mother doesn't lay eggs. Each baby boa is about a foot long and it receives no parental care from its mother – it is on its own from birth and must take care of itself right away, finding food and avoiding predators such as large cats, crocodiles, and humans. When they are fully grown, the babies can expect to reach an average length of 10 feet and weight of 50 pounds.

The Boa I interacted with told me that the spiritual gift of the snake is connectedness, clarity and certainty. As I spoke with him, I felt that the snakes are very grounded and noticed that he had a distinctive "primal alive" presence. He felt very raw and passionate and alive. The snake told me that his lesson is to learn patience through timing and trust. This made sense to me since boas are ambush predators who are willing to position themselves in a concealed location near their intended prey and wait for up to three days to strike when the best opportunity presents itself. The Boa told me that his message to humans is "Don't forget who you are. Remember your roots. Don't try to be what you're not, just be present."

After these experiences and conversations, I have a newfound respect and admiration for snakes. Like most wild animals today, the survival of red tailed boas is threatened and they are in need of conservation help. Many boas are illegally hunted for food and for their skin. And although they are easily bred in captivity, many wild boas are still captured to be sold in the pet trade in the United States. Of course, deforestation in temperate and rain forests continues to destroy their habitats, making it hard for them to survive.

Like the snakes in my dream, all snakes seem to have the stealthy ability to move silently below our radar screens. Unlike cute, cuddly mammals, snakes don't make good poster animals for conservation – they don't elicit the same protective instincts in most people's hearts as baby mammals do. But like all wild animals, they are important components of many ecosystems and, as I am learning through my studies this year, they have important spiritual lessons to learn, lessons that their souls couldn't get in any other form.

BOTTLENOSE DOLPHIN, *Tursiops truncatus*

I've always been in love with marine mammals. From the time I was given my nickname "Seal Baby" when I was three, I've always loved and identified with sea mammals. I saw my first live dolphin at Marine World, a theme park in northern California, when I was in third grade. I fell in love with the dolphins and regularly begged to go back to the park over and over.

One night when I was a junior in high school, my mom took me to see a new documentary film being shown at the Palace of Fine Arts in San Francisco. The film, called "Dolphin," documented the lives of wild spotted dolphins living near the Bahamas. It was the first film by Hardy Jones, a wildlife filmmaker who for nearly thirty years has championed dolphin conservation and worked to stop the brutal annual killing of dolphins in Japan. I was mesmerized by the graceful animals swimming across the screen and I longed to be there, swimming with them in the crystal clear ocean water. After the film ended, there was a question and answer talk with Hardy Jones himself. He told the audience that he needed paying volunteers to join him in the Bahamas next summer to continue his study of these intelligent, playful creatures.

The next summer, I was one of his volunteers – my mom had agreed to pay half my expenses if I paid the other half, which I did with money earned working at a tourist coffee house on the weekends. The week-long trip was capped off by my amazing swim with the group of dolphins that I shared earlier. That was it. I fell for dolphins – hook, line and sinker. My heart, mind and spirit were united in a quest to learn everything there was to know about dolphins. When I got back home, I went to our local public library and read everything about dolphins I could get my hands on. I read all of John Lilly's books and began dreaming about my career studying dolphins.

I would go on to study dolphins for twenty years after that first trip to the Bahamas. As an undergraduate at University of California San Diego, I was a volunteer at Sea World working with sea birds, but I visited the Sea World dolphins each week on my way to or from the sea bird exhibits. I studied mother-infant social development and behavior in captive bottlenose dolphins at, of all places (!), Marine World for my master's thesis. The summer before I finished my master's degree, I returned to the Bahamas to work as a naturalist for a San Francisco-based ecotourism company. I lived on a 70-foot schooner and supported a researcher studying the same dolphins I had swum with more than ten years before. And every day, I swam in those crystal clear waters with those dolphins myself. I never had quite the same experience that I had had with those three dolphins I swam with when I was in high school, but I got to know individual dolphins, watch interactions within the community, and understand the social structure of different groups.

For my PhD dissertation, I studied coastal bottlenose dolphins in South Carolina. I learned about their ranging patterns, interactions, foraging behavior and more. One of the coolest things I got to study was a strand feeding behavior used by some of the dolphins. During low tide when long flat mud banks are exposed in the tidal creeks, some South Carolina dolphins will hurl themselves out of the water to slide onto the land. They create a huge wall of water in front of them. Anything that happens to be in that water gets tossed onto land when the wave breaks on the mud. Mullet have a habit of resting in small ledges on the underwater cliffs in front of the mud banks. They are carried onto the land with the wave of water. The dolphins slide up on the mud, always lying on their right sides, and snatch any fish they can reach. After getting their fill, the dolphins wiggle and slide back into the water. Sometimes, when the conditions are just right, a group of dolphins will strand feed like this dozens of times in an hour.

Yes, I've done my homework on dolphins. That's why I can tell you all the upcoming cool facts about dolphins from both book learning and personal experience. Dolphins are medium-sized marine mammals that live in every temperate and tropical ocean in the world and some rivers. There are forty species of dolphins, from the nearly blind Amazon River dolphin living in freshwater to the dramatic and impressive orca (or killer whale).

Porpoises are not included in this group of marine mammals. Although the names "dolphin" and "porpoise" used to be used interchangeably, today scientists use the names more precisely. What is the difference between dolphins and porpoises? Dolphins and porpoises belong to two different scientific families. The porpoises are in the family Phocoenidae and they tend to be smaller than dolphins with a more blunt face. Their teeth are different, too. Porpoises' teeth are spade shaped (they look like a bunch of little flat, white shovels lined up in the porpoises' mouths) while dolphins teeth are cone-shaped and end in a sharp point. Dolphins belong to the family Delphinidae.

The dolphin that is most familiar to people is the bottlenose dolphin. The TV star Flipper was a bottlenose dolphin and the most common species of the dolphins on display at theme parks and aquaria is the bottlenose dolphin. They evolved 10 million years ago during the early Miocene period. They eat mainly fish and squid. Coastal bottlenose dolphins live in groups averaging twelve individuals, although their group size can vary from a solitary individual to pairs to dozens of dolphins feeding or socializing together for a short time. Threats to dolphins include sharks, pollution, hunting, massive kills in Japan, pesticides in the water and getting caught as by-catch in tuna and other fisheries.

Living in the water presents special physiological challenges for dolphins. Light doesn't reach far into the water so dolphins have developed extra sensitive eyes as well as their famous echolocation ability. A well-developed, specialized layer of cells at the back of the eye called the *tapetum lucidum* reflects light through the retina a second time giving dolphins twice as much light to use to see as humans. (Many nocturnal animals, such as cats and owls, also have this adaptation. You can tell an animal has this special reflective layer when their eyes seem to glow at night.)

Sonar clicks emitted from the dolphin's melon (the fatty bulb of flesh on the forehead) bounce back to the dolphin when they strike an object. From this echo, dolphins can create a mental image of the landscape in front of them. Dolphins send and receive many clicks per second to create a detailed picture of their surroundings even in complete darkness. Echolocation is an active sense: dolphins must use it consciously. Thus, echolocation "hearing" and "seeing" is not always "on." This may be one of the reasons that dolphins become accidentally entangled in fishing gear. It may be that they can detect the gear, but they are not always "looking" for it and therefore get tangled in it.

Just as dogs can smell much better than humans because they have more nerve fibers for smelling, dolphins can hear much better than humans for the same reason. The dolphin's auditory cortex, the part of the brain that controls hearing, has roughly twice as many nerve fibers as a human's. Dolphins hear best between 40 and 100 kHz but they can hear sounds in a wide range of frequencies, from 1 to 150 kHz. The human hearing range is from 0.02 to 17 kHz.

Hydrodynamic streamlining for life in the water eliminated the dolphin's external ear but dolphins can still hear very well. They have two small external ear openings that look like pin holes, one behind each eye. Through their ears, dolphins can probably hear sounds at the lower end of their hearing range. They also have a specialized hearing system, with broad sound receptors on each side of the head and insulated inner ears that receive sound from only one source. This set-up allows dolphins to localize sounds underwater very effectively, an almost impossible task for human swimmers. They actually hear through their lower jaw. Huh? How do they do that? The lower jawbone is hollow and becomes broad where it hinges with the skull. A very thin bone extends back toward the bone that encases the inner ear. Fibrous tissues surround this connection, buffering the inner ear from the skull. Water-borne sounds are received most efficiently by specialized fat in the lower jaw and fat extending from the jaw to the inner ear conducts the sound to the ear. The sound is then conducted by nerves from the ear to hearing centers in the brain by the auditory nerve.

A surprising challenge that dolphins face living in the ocean is water conservation. Because ocean water is saltier than the dolphins' blood, it tends to suck water out of the dolphins' bodies. Dolphins have no way to drink fresh water to maintain their internal water-salt balance, so water conservation is as important to dolphins as it is to desert animals. Through special adaptations in their bodies, dolphins are able to get all the water they need from the food they eat, the air they breathe, and from breaking down stored fat in their bodies. They also have specialized kidneys (that look like a sack of grapes) that retain as much water as possible, producing urine that is saltier than seawater.

See? I've learned a lot about dolphins! But before I get carried away with scientific knowledge, let's look at the ways that humans viewed dolphins over the centuries. Racing alongside a boat or leaping in front of the setting sun, dolphins have been capturing human hearts for eons. Humans have probably been fascinated by dolphins for as long as our two species have coexisted. Firmly rooted in our collective consciousness, dolphins have appeared in our art, myths, and literature for millennia. Dolphins seem to embody all the traits that humans have and those to which we aspire. Their graceful form and joyful athleticism win over our hearts whether we are three or ninety-three.

Ancient and modern sailors believe that dolphins riding on the bow of a ship are a good omen. To early Christians, dolphins were a symbol of salvation. Dolphins were the messengers of Poseidon, the Greek god of the sea. Ancient Maoris also believed that dolphins were the messengers of the gods. Pre-Hellenic Greeks worshipped dolphins as gods themselves. In Native American traditions, dolphins symbolize the breath of life and the life force. The Boto dolphins in the Amazon River are believed by locals to be shape shifters who are capable of having children with human women.

When I was in the middle of a year of intensive psychic training a few years ago, I had the great pleasure of learning how to astral travel in a safe, protected way. On one of my in-class journeys, I got the opportunity to meet one of my spirit guides. He is a dolphin spirit guide whose job is to help me communicate with dolphins. When it came time to write this chapter, I contacted this guide and asked him my three questions. According to my dolphin spirit guide, the spiritual gift of the dolphin is deep love and joy. My guide goes on to explain that dolphins are a mind in the waters – beings with a similarly high level of consciousness as humans but living in a different medium than ours. They are similar in consciousness to humans but they have different types of experiences because of their slightly different brain, physical make up, and anatomy. Dolphins get the full range of human experiences in a different world with different outcomes. Their spiritual lessons and experiences are similar or on par with ours, but with a watery twist that makes things a little bit different.

My guide told me that the spiritual lesson of dolphins is to experience a higher consciousness in a denser medium and to learn to live with the limitations inherent in physical life. "Although we experience energy with more awareness than humans, we are still limited by our physical restrictions. We are still in a dense body in a dense medium. We are here to work through our range of emotional/spiritual lessons, too, like humans, but we have higher consciousness in a denser medium and that produces serious limitations. We learn to live with those limitations."

The message that dolphins have for humans is to deepen into our souls and feel the joy that is our natural birthright. As my guide put it, "Joy. Have more joy. Enjoy yourselves more. Deepen into your soul and feel the joy that is your natural birthright. Live from there and all will be okay. You can face anything from this place. It's available to you all the time, just tune into it."

Whether in a movie, a photo or in person, dolphins have the power to ignite a primordial love and appreciation in humans. They seem to touch us deeply and it always seems to be positive. Dolphins represent all that is good in the world and they seem to embody all the positive traits we want to see in ourselves. They remind us to have fun and to be centered in our souls and live from that place of expansiveness and freedom. Dolphins are probably the animal closest to us in consciousness, our closest spiritual kin. As our brothers and sisters of the deep, I'd like to provide them a cleaner home and fewer intrusions from boats and industry. As a mind in the waters, I want to learn more about what it's like to be such an aware being living in such an alien environment. For me, this was just the first contact with dolphin souls. I hope to create a lot more connections with them in the future. They are complex creatures, just like us, and one visit is not enough, certainly not for this lifelong dolphin lover. I'll be back, my friends, I'll be back.

A Dolphin is Born
Pulses of energy. Pulses of light.
Everything is rhythm.
Pause and rest. Begin again.
Beating tail, take a breath.
Pop and whoosh. Pop and whoosh.
Released from gravity. Released from sound. Released from earth.
Back inside – feel the pressure, feel the sound, feel the energy all
around.
Mystical musical dancing around.
Looking, wondering all around.
Feel the voices. Hear them in each cell.
Feel the vibration calling out a knell.
Calling to the Earth, calling to the Sky; feeling the water pushing me
high.
Hear the voices, feel the sound - energy bouncing all around.
Feel the circle around you – aunts and uncles join in the dance,
thank the heavens: here's another chance.
Feel the light, see the sounds.
Souls are living all around.
Feel the earth, the energy cocoon,
within the Field, under the moon.
Light shining down, dispersing in the depths,
Lines and shadows, merging into one,
One dance of light, of love, of life.
Lines and shadows, dancing in the depths,
Giving connections between the surface and the depths.
Lines and shadows, silence and sound,
Merging into oneness all around.

Part Three: Now and Into the Future

.

Living My Truth

Animal Insights

As I wrote in the Testing My Truth chapter, all science begins with a question. A scientist asks herself, what am I curious about? Then she rearranges her interest into a hypothesis. My hypothesis for this book was that animals are spiritual beings with their unique curriculum (spiritual lessons) and gifts (service to the planet). I asked each animal I encountered the same three questions: What is your spiritual lesson? What is your spiritual gift? Do you have a message you want to share with humans? I chose these three questions because it seemed to me that the answers that animals would give me would either support or refute my hypothesis.

If animals didn't have a spiritual lesson or gift, then they would have answered me in very different ways than they did. They might have said something like "Huh? What are you talking about?" or "Just give me the kibble and nobody gets hurt" or something like that. But they didn't. They knew exactly what I was asking them. They knew why they were here. I was communicating with them on the soul level and their souls knew what they were here to do. Based on my conversations and experiences with all the different animals I connected with this year, I have to accept my hypothesis and conclude that animals are spiritual beings with their unique curriculum (spiritual learning) and gifts (service to the planet).

Early in the writing of this book, after interviewing animals from more than twenty different species and asking them my three questions, I was asked, "What has been the biggest surprise?" What a great question! Each animal has touched me deeply, but the biggest surprise for me was my experience with the bats. The reality of their life experience and their awareness of each other, the devotion and connection among the group members was astounding to me. The love and acceptance was palpable to me and everything about that experience was almost the exact opposite of everything that I had read or seen or heard about bats. It was the antithesis of how bats are portrayed in movies, just for starters. I fell in love with bats that day by the bridge and I didn't expect that at all.

The great gray owl was another revelation for me. The empathy and wisdom of that bird was profound. I was struck by the possibility that nothing is the way I think it is. Maybe there are spiritual sentinels of other species that are watching over the earth. If so, the owl must surely be one of them. The owl has helped me in my own life to make hard choices and to accept my power in doing so. The owl has helped me have clarity and strength and accept the consequences of my choices.

The messages from the elephant and the whale were the most touching to me. As large, roaming animals who need lots of space and freedom, I mourned the restrictions humans have imposed on them and the loss of their way of life at our hands. The anger of the elephants is justified, in my opinion.

The dolphin's message, of course, is close to my heart and a great reminder that we have the power to choose our experience in each moment. Each animal's gift or lesson or message touched me and in each one I find words that remind who I am and why I'm here. Each animal faces situations and lessons that I, too, face in my own way. I find myself remembering their words at different times and using them as guides for my own thinking and behavior. For me, though, the greatest gift has been the brief moments of connection between our souls. Those moments confirmed for me my lifelong belief that we are all one; that we are all truly connected.

Two ways of seeing

Scientists are like Missouri, the Show Me State. Scientists say "I'll believe it when I see it." Spiritual traditions, however, are the opposite. They promote an "I'll see it when I believe it" frame of mind. I've lived in both of these states and although each group probably would argue that their way of seeing the world is more correct than the other, I can see that both ways are right. I have had experiences when something had to be proven to me before I would believe that it was true. But I've also had experiences that because I believed in them I got to experience them. The two ways of seeing seem contradictory, but I see them as complimentary.

The beauty of science to me is distilling love and curiosity into a question that you can ask the world and get an answer. I think our most natural state as humans is to be curious. Kids love learning things. Babies love learning things – they focus and concentrate harder than any other group of humans I know. We love to learn. And we love to learn about things that we love. Why is a tree green? Why does a dolphin leap in the ocean? At its best, scientific inquiry comes from someone loving something so much that they are curious about it and want to learn more. And science is all about questions, questions formed in a way that the scientist can observe or measure something in order to answer their question and satisfy their curiosity.

When I was working on my master's degree, I could think of no better way to spend my time than watching dolphins and learning about them. I read everything about dolphins that I could get my hands on, watched every movie and tv show I knew about, volunteered for anything dolphin-related, including investigating a large dolphin die-off in Texas. I was in love with dolphins. I loved dolphins more than any other animal in the world and more than any other activity in the world. They were my everything.

I was curious about everything that had anything to do with dolphins and everything I learned stuck in my mind. I learned about kidneys because dolphins have very cool kidneys (they look like a sack of grapes, not at all like a human's kidney bean shaped kidney). I learned about ocean currents and salinity and mineral content and upwelling because these were things that affected dolphins. I learned a lot about plants in my science classes, and I couldn't tell you one thing today that I learned about plants but if I heard something or read it once about dolphins, that was it: it was in my brain forever.

I loved dolphins so much and was so curious about them that I spent nearly twenty years asking question after question about them in different scientific studies. I spent six years and more than 120,000 hours studying dolphins for my PhD dissertation alone. This is what I mean that the beauty of science to me is distilling love and curiosity into a question that you can ask the world and get an answer.

For this book, I combined my love of animals and my curiosity about the spiritual make up of our world into a scientific framework that would help me understand both better. I took a spiritual question and applied the scientific method to it. As I integrated science and spirituality in my work, I also integrated it in myself.

Integrating science and spirit

For most of my life, I bounced back and forth between phases that I labeled "scientific" and "spiritual." School was a "science" phase for me, from high school through my doctoral program. Between academic degrees, I often felt I was in a more "spiritual" phase of my life. This is when I had time to meditate or take classes on consciousness or the human energy system or visit my local Zen Center for a dharma talk. The quality of my life was different during these two different phases. Neither was better or worse, but they felt different to me. The scientific phase was intellectual and questing and doing. The spiritual phase was opening and being and experiencing and feeling.

By my mid-thirties, I yearned for integration. I felt like I was choosing one or the other. I had one foot in the spiritual world and one foot in the scientific world and I wanted to live a balanced life with both feet on the ground at the same time. I also had a lot of judgments about the other phase – whichever one I was in at the time was the "good" phase and the other was "bad." I felt like I had to choose between the two. When I was with scientists, I felt I had to hide my spiritual side and when I was with spiritual people they looked at me like I was talking gibberish when I used words that were even remotely scientific-sounding. My life became "either or" and "bad or good."

In October, when I began this project, I still felt that I was out of balance and that both parts of myself were not equally represented. My life felt compartmentalized. I wanted to celebrate what I saw as both sides of my brain: my left brain that was logical and linear and great for evaluating information and critical thinking and my right brain that held my imagination, my intuition, my creativity, and my ability to love and empathize with people. But I wasn't doing it yet. It took almost a year of consciously using both sides of my brain to see how they work together, how they integrate with each other and support each other.

Now, I see both aspects of my being as good. I have two distinct tools, each good in its own circumstances. They can support and enhance each other. From science, I've learned how to create structure and method, discernment and evaluation, objectivity and curiosity, and how to be very specific. In scientific speaking and writing, you can only say what your data supports and you learn how to be very accurate and specific in what you say and how you say it. From my spirituality, I've learned love and openness, subjectivity and curiosity, synthesis and making connections. As I was writing this book, I outlined the animal chapter using mind maps to brain storm and find connections, which comes from my right brain, and I used a standard, numbered outline when I started writing this chapter. When I chose my three questions, I used my left brain and scientific training to distill down the relevant information that I wanted to learn into my questions. I also used my right brain, as I asked myself "what feels meaningful to me?" I feel like my whole process has helped me integrate and become aware of the integration of both parts of my brain and my psyche.

My three questions

During the writing of my animal chapters, I started really getting into my three questions. I had asked the same question to dozens of animals and had gotten surprising answers from most of them. Patterns were emerging and I was beginning to feel like I had a sense of some spiritual organization in the world. The more I pondered the animals' answers, the more intrigued I became about my own line of inquiry. It suddenly struck me as funny that I had all this information from animals, but I'd never asked my three questions to a person. "Huh! I should do that! That would be interesting!" I thought to myself. Then I had to ask myself who would have intriguing answers to my questions. It would have to be somebody thoughtful and spiritual . . . my teachers!

At a lunch break during our class in April, I asked my Spiritual Psychology teacher at USM Dr. Ron Hulnick my three questions. Ron shared that his spiritual gift is "the ability to transmute challenging principles into understandable concepts, to make things more understandable. Like an artist sees a vision and translates it into form or reality, I do the same for concepts." I remarked that he did this not just for concepts, but also experiences, giving people a spiritual and practical context in which to interpret and understand their experiences and Ron agreed with me.

When I asked Ron what his spiritual lesson or challenge is, he replied, "I used to be very angry and had a lot of rules about the way things should be and what was wrong with everyone. All of that had to go. That was my lesson."

Ron's message to people is that "You didn't do anything wrong. Everyone is inherently worthy regardless of what they've thought or done – whether they believe it or not." He really wants people to understand and know this at the deepest level possible. As he repeatedly says in class, "God allows everything. How do we know this? Because it occurs. If God didn't want it to happen, it wouldn't happen. So, there is nothing that you can do that is not allowed by God." So many of us are beating ourselves up for something we thought or did that we judge ourselves for or think that we are unworthy or unlovable for doing or thinking. Ron's message is that we are here to learn that we are all worthy and all loveable by virtue of the fact that we exist. It's that simple.

After I talked to Ron, I got curious about how other spiritual teachers would see themselves and their spiritual journey in this lifetime. I'd like to keep asking my three questions to more animals and people, but that will be another book. The process, though, made me think about my own life and my spiritual journey. So, I asked myself my three questions. When I did, that same weekend in April, I was actually surprised by my answers.

When I asked myself what my spiritual gift is, I felt my answer on two levels. I see my primary gift as loving -- loving myself and loving my family, especially my kids. I am here to be a battery of love for everyone that I encounter. At another level, I see my spiritual gift as the synthesis of many skills. It is the ability to access and present spiritual experiences and information in a way that allows other people to access their own spiritual truth.

When I look back at earlier painful episodes in my life from my current perspective and place of peace, I see that my spiritual challenge or lesson was (and continues to be) knowing who I am and loving myself no matter what. This means knowing my true, authentic self and loving myself whether or not I am receiving love or appreciation or approval from someone else. Many of the most painful moments in my life emerged from judgments I made against myself as not smart or pretty or friendly or artistic or whatever enough. I looked outside myself for approval and for proof of my worth and value. Sometimes I got it, sometimes I didn't. But as look back now, I see each quest for approval as an opportunity to love myself and to give myself what I had been looking for from someone else. My lesson is to love myself the way I want to be loved, to love myself the way I love my friends and family – wholly, completely and unconditionally.

My message to people in its simplest terms is: "We are love. We are all connected. We are one." The way I see it, our very essence is love. That's what we are made of, whether we are a good person or not, whether we are a nice person or not, and whether we are a person or a snake or a whale. We are all made of the same energy and that energy is love. There is no difference between me and you and a polar bear. We are all the same, energetically and spiritually. We are not only connected to each other, but we are one.

A new paradigm

Why do I identify so much with animals and why do I love them so much? And it's not just me. Americans spend billions of dollars on their pets each year. We love animals. What attracts humans to animals? E.O. Wilson, the eminent Harvard University sociobiologist and author, believes that there is a genetic basis for our love of animals, something embedded in the very cells of our bodies that drives us to touch and interact with wild and domesticated animals. He calls this inherent tendency to focus on and affiliate with other beings "biophilia" or "love of life" or "love of living things." According to Wilson, our relationships with animals form a fundamental part of our existence.

My scientific and spiritual experiences converged to show me that not only are we attracted to animals but we are animals. Our biological make up is almost identical to all other animals on this planet. We share the same genes with chimpanzees, which is no surprise, but we share the same genes with mice and octopi and other animals. The small differences that define species come down not to differences in our DNA but differences in whether specific genes in our DNA are activated or not. Spiritually, we are the same, too. We are each here to learn our own spiritual curriculum. Which school we go to determines our species – our souls learn different lessons when we're a snake than when we're a whale. Our spiritual curriculum determines what life form our soul will take.

I look at my world now as one of many dimensions. One dimension is the regular reality that I've always known. Overlapped with that reality is my new spiritual reality. Overlapping both of those is the reality of each animal or species of animal that exists and shares the same space. When I go running in the park and see a lizard, our realities overlap and two dimensions are present. I see the world from my perspective as a five foot three and a half inch woman moving quickly down a trail. The lizard sees the world from much closer to the ground and perceives different aspects of the environment – the movement of the grass, sounds in a certain range of frequencies. Birds flying overhead are beautiful to me but dangerous to the lizard. And yet, the lizard is also learning spiritual lessons in this lifetime just like me. The lizard is made of the same raw materials as me chemically, biologically and spiritually.

We are all the same. We are one.

When I began working on this project last October, I was pushing myself way out of my comfort zone and I was filled with insecurities and doubts. My inner conversation went something like this: Who am I to write a book about communicating with animals? I've barely just begun to do it myself! I don't know what I'm doing! I'm not a great, talented psychic! I'm not a great, talented scientist! I'm certainly not a great, talented spiritual teacher! Who am I to investigate the spiritual make up of our world using the scientific method?

Then the words of Marianne Williamson floated through my head. She said, "Who am I to be brilliant, gorgeous, talented and fabulous? Actually, who are you not to be? You are a child of God. Your playing small doesn't serve the world." And she was right. Part of my journey this year was reclaiming my self-confidence and gaining new confidence in myself and my abilities, my ability to communicate intuitively with animals, my ability to write a compelling book, my ability to harness my curiosity about the world and give it a structure for asking clear, answerable questions.

I was particularly struck by something that Maya Angelou, one my heroes, said. She said she doesn't like humble people, she thinks they're fakes. "I know that whatever I have is a gift," she says. "I accept that and I'm grateful to those who went before me so that I can do what I'm supposed to do for those who are yet to come. That's humility." Before I read these words, I had thought that being self-effacing and downplaying my gifts and abilities was showing humility. Now I understand that owning my gifts and abilities is true humility. It's not coming from my ego, there is no judgment saying that I am better or worse than anyone else, there is simply an acceptance and an owning of who I really am.

I heard these words from these wise women and they comforted and inspired me and I understood them intellectually, but I had to earn my gut understanding of them over several months and years. Through the many hours that I have spent intuitively communicating with animals and writing drafts of this book, I have earned my humility, my awareness that I have gifts to share and these are two of them. Because that comes from within and I give it to myself, I don't need to look outside for reassurance. I don't need approval or understanding from anyone else.

So now I find myself with a new paradigm of the world, one that is very eye-opening and empowering. We are all (humans and animals alike) spiritual beings with unique lessons and gifts. What do I do with my new paradigm? How do I live in a world that I understand to be filled with divine beings having unique earth experiences in order to learn spiritual lessons? There are no easy answers to these questions, no guidelines to follow like a prescription or a diet for spiritual growth. The Sanskrit greeting "Namaste," which means the divine in me recognizes and salutes the divine in you, is a place to start. From here, with each being I encounter, human or animal, I recognize that there is a soul inside that being that is the same as my soul. I try to live from a place that says "let peace begin with me." I try to recognize that soul and treat it with the respect that each soul deserves. For me, this simple guideline is the only one that can help me with the myriad interactions and choices I make each day.

So, if you find yourself asking yourself how to move forward with the knowledge and insight you've gained from this book, remember that you were born to shine, too. We are all divine beings. Just like I did, you will have to leave your comfort zone and follow your intuition into uncharted territory. Sometimes, I have to follow it minute by minute because I don't have my old general guidelines any more. The old rules and beliefs I used to live by don't fit me anymore. I created them before I had this understanding about the world, before I understood that I am here to learn spiritual lessons and to share my gifts, before I learned that animals are here to learn their spiritual lessons and share their gifts.

You are here to learn your spiritual lessons and share your gifts. You are powerful beyond measure. You have the strength and the clarity and the power to make your choices from this informed place. If you choose to stop eating meat, great. If you choose to keep eating meat, great. Like the great gray owl, we make our choices, the ones that are right for us, and we accept the consequences of our actions. That is the way of the world. There is no one right answer for the millions of choices we each make in our lives. Together we can create the way as we move forward in this new paradigm.

Each chapter of this book focuses on one species of animal. Taken together, these pieces show us a larger picture, a picture of interlocking pieces. We are all tied together on so many levels. We are all made of the same atoms and molecules and the same spiritual building blocks of energy and spirit. Our biological systems and chemical reactions in our bodies are the same. Physically, we are all very similar even if our bodies appear different-looking. Spiritually, the same is true. We should treasure each variation on Spirit's theme of perfection. Then we can truly have a heaven on earth. Each of us is a unique, valuable piece of the puzzle that is our world. Let's celebrate that.

Namaste.

Table of Spiritual Messages

Animal	Gift	Lesson	Message
Dog	love and devotion	nothing when alone	play!
Elephant	traditions	integrating old and new	no compromise
Horse	love, power, partnership	powerful but dependent	open your heart to let someone in
Bat	collective consciousness	never alone, selflessness	The whole is greater than the sum of the parts
Snake	connectedness, primal aliveness	patience, timing, trust	don't try to be what you're not
Whale	equanimity, present moment	cycles and surrender	love and care for oceans
Owl	clarity of vision, knowledge and action	unbearable compassion	take care of self and accept consequences
Cat	sleek, swift, focused hunter	balancing autonomy and interdependence	give us what we want, then leave us alone
African Lion	doing it all decisive leadership	surrender, endure; good times will end	do what you're called to do; be as great as you dream
Dolphin	deep love and joy	higher consciousness in denser medium - limits	deepen into your soul and feel the joy

Suggested Reading

Animal Omens by Victoria Hunt is lovely little book that combines
true stories about animal encounters with ancient
symbolic wisdom about each creature's meaning.

Animal Speak by Ted Andrews is an extensive encyclopedia of the
symbolism of mammals, birds and reptiles and
amphibians in Native American traditions.

Animals Make Us Human by Temple Grandin, PhD relates the
author's understanding of each animal as well as the
bonds between humans and animals.

The Biology of Belief by Bruce Lipton, PhD explores the interface of
cell biology and spiritual reality and how this
awareness can help us create our own futures.

Biophilia by E. O. Wilson, PhD details Dr. Wilson's theory of our
innate love of all living things.

Journey of Souls by Michael Newton, PhD expands the frontiers in
our understanding of the time between lives and the
spiritual organization of our universe.

Learning Their Language by Marta Williams is a wonderful
exploration of communication with all kinds of
animals and nature.

Loyalty to Your Soul by Ron and Mary Hulnick explains Spiritual
Psychology as a way to use every day experiences to
advance your spiritual evolution in consciousness.

Medicine Cards by Jamie Sams and David Carson details the
meaning of forty-four animals in Native American

spiritual traditions to accompany the Medicine Cards deck.

Straight from the Horse's Mouth by Amelia Kinkade is a delightful book that explores the author's intuitive conversations and experiences with a variety of animals.

You Are Psychic by Debra Lynn Katz is a practical and inspiring guide to developing your own psychic abilities, including insightful stories and helpful exercises.

Acknowledgments

The first draft of this book was written as part of my Second Year Project for my Master's Degree in Spiritual Psychology at the University of Santa Monica. I truly don't think this book would ever have come even close to materializing without this amazing school and it certainly wouldn't have done so in such a beautiful, graceful, and Spirit-filled way in a matter of nine short months. I am grateful to everyone at USM, especially faculty Drs. Ron and Mary Hulnick and Dr. David Paul, and all the volunteers and assistants throughout both years of the program. Thank you to Jonathan Brennan for being the first to model the USM principles and a new way of being in the world and inspiring me to embark on this new adventure. Thanks to both Skip Downing and Jonathan Brennan for encouraging me to attend USM and for being great people to work with. I cherish the many hours we spent working, talking and laughing together. I am ever grateful to my project team, Aleya Coolidge, Anne Marie Arrow and Lisa Jones, for their love, support, inspiration, encouragement and understanding. All of my USM classmates contributed to this book through their presence and support in class and out and for sharing themselves so openly and honestly, creating a safe space for me to do the same. Thank you to Edie and Renee for fun Saturday lunches that led to true friendship. Deep, deep thanks to Debra, Eric, Molly, Aleya, Dennis and Rebekah for graciously letting me invade their homes for long USM weekends. Thank you to Bruce Harnishfeger for allowing me to include his beautiful poem, written while we were students together at USM.

Thanks to Margaret VanLaanMartin, my psychic teacher, for giving me the skills and structure I needed to train my natural abilities into something useful and meaningful. Thanks to Ellery Moon for being my "partner in crime" from the beginning as I began to explore this topic and my intuitive abilities. Thanks to Ellery, Shardel, Edie, and Renee for memorable trips to the Sacramento and San Diego Zoos. My good friends in Chico, Ellery, Michele, Whitney, and Analia, loved and supported me throughout this adventure. True friends, they have made my life rich and fun and loving and have given me a sense of community and sisterhood. You are the best!

My world begins and ends with my family. Chris, Lexi, Zane, and Iko, you make every day a joy and I love sharing it all with each of you. Thank you for loving me just the way I am and for sharing the beauty of your true selves with me day in and day out and in good moods and in bad. I love you more than my words could ever express. Erika and Wendy, you are part of my family of the heart. Thank you for being my friends for all these years and across all these miles. We are connected in heart and soul where distance doesn't exist. Thank you for being you and for sharing you with me. Mom and Dad, it all began with you and I thank you both from the bottom of my heart for being my parents and loving and supporting me in all that I do. I love you.

Thank you to all the animals that connected with me and thank you to all the clients who have allowed me to enter their worlds through their pets. Thank you to everyone who has been a part of my journey to write this book. I love you all!

About the Author

Cara believes that all beings are divine beings and when we recognize ourselves as divine and all the beings around us as divine, we live in a world that is a better place for everyone.

Cara Gubbins, Ph.D., began conducting scientific research as a high school student in 1981. She received her doctorate in Ecology, Evolution and Conservation Biology in 2000 from the University of Nevada Reno. Cara and her research have been featured on CNN, the BBC, the Discovery Channel, and National Geographic Specials.

Dr. Gubbins is the author of the award-winning book *The Dolphins of Hilton Head ~ Their Natural History*, a non-fiction book for adults. She has published numerous articles in local, regional, and international magazines, celebrated the natural world in her *Naturally Speaking* newspaper column in the (Hilton Head) Island Packet, and is the co-author of *Power Stories ~ Everyday Women Creating Extraordinary Lives*.

Cara lives with her husband, their two children, and their Australian shepherds in northern California. Professionally, she helps connect people to animals, nature and Spirit through intuitive readings, coaching and classes, as well as international spiritual retreats, while specializing in intuitive communication with animals.

You can learn more about Cara and her coaching, retreats and intuitive readings at www.caragubbins.com.

Made in the USA
Columbia, SC
10 December 2023

28195922R00085